Helena Haraštová & Jana Sedláčková

ATLAS OF CATS

Illustrations by Giulia Lombardo

KEEP CALM AND
ADOPT A CAT

This book is dedicated
to all cat lovers!

Albatros

TABLE OF CONTENTS

INTRODUCTION

All cats and kittens love to play and sleep—did you know they sleep through almost *three quarters* of their life?!—and often they're quite stubborn . . . unless they consume catnip, which entices them to roll around and act silly. Simply put, cats are quite the characters. Also . . .

They're huge rascals!

. . . But at the same time they're the cutest pets around.

They love helping us . . . and sometimes just watching what we're doing.

Deep inside, they're little predators—and no wonder, since they count wild lions, tigers, pumas, and leopards among their relatives! They began palling around with us humans as early as almost 10,000 years ago.

They love hearth and home. They also enjoy playing hide-and-seek in cramped spaces, where they pretty much just melt into taking a nap.

CATS ARE INCREDIBLE, MYSTERIOUS CREATURES . . . HERE'S WHY.

🐾 My excellent sight allows me to see in the dark, six times better than humans. My eyes reflect all of the available light, which makes them look like they're shining in the dark!

🐾 I explore my surroundings with my whiskers. They also help me find my bearings when it's pitch dark.

🐾 My rough tongue is a bit scratchy. I use it mainly to groom my coat (which I spend approximately 15% of my time doing). It can also scrape meat off of bones like a tiny grater.

🐾 My ears are moved by 32 muscles and I can turn them 180 degrees. They can hear even the quietest mice in the world.

🐾 My strong legs and flexible spine, made from 53 loosely moving vertebrae, allow me to jump at distances six times the length of my body. And I almost always land on my feet! That's due to the stabilization system in my inner ear.

🐾 I communicate my mood by changing the position of my tail. Right now, I'm happy you're reading about me!

🐾 There's a unique pattern on my nose, just like you humans have unique fingerprints. By sniffing around, I learn about my surroundings and meet other cats.

🐾 My sensitive paws with retractable claws are covered with soft pads that drain sweat away from my body.

🐾 I have around 40 million hairs!

THE MYSTERY OF FELINE PURRING AND MEOWING

Cats came up with meowing to communicate with us people. They also make one other peculiar sound, and that's purring. Why they do this remains a mystery. Sometimes, they use it to let us know how much they like that belly rub we're giving them. But many scientists also believe they purr to calm themselves down when they're afraid or hurting.

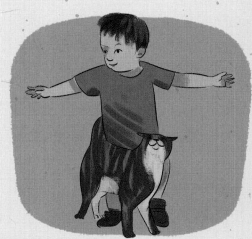

YOU ARE A PART OF MY TERRITORY!

Has a cat ever rubbed her cheeks or tail on you? She did it to put her scent on you and mark you as a rightful member of her territory!

EUROPEAN SHORTHAIR

Despite what you might believe, a savage beast still lives deep inside me—and so I sometimes miss the times when I could run freely in the wild. Crouch, turn my ears up, extend my claws . . . and pounce!

CRAFTY LITTLE MOUSER

APPEARANCE

STRONG MUSCLED BODY WITH A SHORT THICK COAT

TEMPERAMENT

Each one of us cats is unique. That's because we are not usually bred, and unlike other breeds, we don't have to meet strict rules on personality and temperament. We tend to be smart (naturally), playful, and energetic, but we're not hotheads. An afternoon snooze on a windowsill? Yes please. What we really love, though, is hunting—those instincts are very strong.

ROUND HEAD WITH FULL CHEEKS

STRONG LEGS WITH ROUND PAWS

HOW i FiRST SAW THE LiGHT OF DAY

The first humans I ever befriended were the Roman soldiers I accompanied on their journey around Europe, protecting their food supplies from hungry rodents and cheeky birds. I can't even describe the respect they showed me! Over time, I stopped being a wild predator and turned into a loyal domestic companion, as well as the terror of all mice that infest pantries and storerooms. ➡

WHO ARE YOU, iNTRUDER?

Just like wild animals defend their territory, so do I fight for the right to rule my home. Over time, I may come to accept a new cat or dog friend, but it usually takes me a while. After all, I must make sure that my human pack still loves me, since our house is so crowded all of a sudden!

INTERESTING FACT

Any household cat that has the appearance and temperament described above can be called a European shorthair, though it's true that such a cat is pretty hard to find in village squares or animal shelters.

OTHER CATS WiTH TABBY PATTERNS

1. Chinese Li Hua
2. Australian Mist
3. Desert Lynx Cat
4. American Shorthair
5. Mojave Spotted Cat
6. Highlander Shorthair

HOW COULD ANYONE GET US MIXED UP?

HIGHLANDER SHORTHAIR

A short tail and upturned ears, as if they've been propped up—you won't mistake me for any other breed.

CHINESE LI HUA

My name combines the Mandarin words for "fox" and "flower." That's because I look pretty wild and my coat's pattern resembles flowers.

DESERT LYNX CAT

I have a funny short tail and an endless list of admirers.

AUSTRALIAN MIST

I'm the very first cat ever bred in Australia.

MOJAVE SPOTED CAT

Up until 1984, we lived only in the wild, deep in the dens of the Mojave Desert.

AMERICAN SHORTHAIR

I arrived in America on European colonial ships, where I hunted rats.

MEOW NEWS

114th YEAR — No. 1363 SINCE 1892 ✿ WEDNESDAY, JULY 12, 2006 ✿ PRICE: 25 CAT HAIRS

A PRIVATE EYE IS WATCHING OVER THE DARK STREETS OF BROOKLYN

TODAY'S EDITION OF THE DAILY CAT BRINGS YOU AN ACCOUNT OF A PRESS CONFERENCE WITH FRED, A TABBY SHORTHAIR TOMCAT WHO WORKED HIS WAY UP FROM BEING A SICK, HOMELESS ORPHAN TO BECOMING A MEMBER OF THE NEW YORK CITY POLICE DEPARTMENT, WHERE HE'S EMPLOYED AS A SECRET AGENT.

Editor Snowball: What is it like, being a secret agent? Is it dangerous?
Fred: Suspenseful. Dangerous. Nerve-racking. But even when the going gets tough, you always know that you're doing the right thing.

Editor Snowball: Tell us more about that. What was the last case you worked?
Fred: There was this guy, a real inconspicuous one. He pretended to be a vet. He had no certification, no credentials, but also no one had any hard evidence connecting him to the crime. Our guys were constantly prowling beneath his windows, looking through the keyhole, but still couldn't catch him in the act. Finally, me and my partner, Stephanie Green-Jones, decided to go undercover. But of course, a vet needs a patient . . .

Editor Snowball: So you volunteered as bait?
Fred: Yep.

Editor Snowball: That's really admirable! (Fred and the editor high-five each other, ed. note)
Fred: *Purrr* . . . All it took was a bit of gumption. When he was just about to inject me with who knows what, Green-Jones leapt to my aid. *Meow!* When we later inspected the crime scene, we found a small cubbyhole in the back, full of animals he wanted to steal.

Editor Snowball: But now the perpetrator is safely locked away.
Fred: Yeah, and . . . I decided to hang up my career as a policeman and become a teacher. Tomorrow is my first day at school. We'll be teaching kids how to handle animals well and with care.

Editor Snowball: Thank you for the interview.

Let's say goodbye to the James Bond of the cat world and wish him many more adventures out there!

BRiTiSH SHORTHAiR

Give me a comfortable couch, the company of a beloved human, and the opportunity to do the occasional feline romping, and I'll be the happiest, most beloved member of your family!

KEEP CALM AND LOVE ME

INTELLIGENCE: 🐾🐾🐾🐾🐾
STUBBORNNESS: 🐾🐾🐾🐾🐾
PERSONALITY: I leave the couch only when I want to play.
WANDERLUST: Where would I go?
CUDDLINESS: Extremely, but only when I want to.

TEMPERAMENT

People love my laid-back nature. I'm a stalwart cool kitty who won't let anything throw her off and willingly pals around both with young human and canine roomies. Feline games and romping are my thing, but I don't need a garden or much space to enjoy myself—I can rule a tiny flat just fine. Preferably from your lap, of course.

APPEARANCE

ROUND HEAD WITH ROUND, USUALLY YELLOW EYES

PLUSH COAT THAT JUST BEGS FOR CUDDLING - -

STRONG, SQUAD BUILD - -

HOW I SAW THE LIGHT OF DAY ➡

My ancestors are said to have been brought to Britain by Ancient Romans. After spending many centuries in the isolation of the British Isles (and catching millions of mice), these queens of the English streets were bred with Persian cats. And voilà—the oldest British breed ever was born. Later, we were once again crossbred with Chartreux cats. That's why we resemble them so much.

⬅ INTERESTING FACT

My sister—the British longhair—has a few more Persian genes than I do and adores logic puzzles.

BRITISH SHORTHAIR COLOR VARIETIES

1. Tri Color—Calico (with green eyes)
2. Blue (traditional)
3. Silver & white (with green eyes)
4. Fawn
5. Chocolate (with golden eyes)
6. Black (with blue eyes)

HOW COULD ANYONE GET US MIXED UP?

↑

KORAT

In Thailand, my home, people believe I bring luck. That's why they often give me to newlyweds as a present.

CHARTREUX CAT ➡

I'm said to have been raised by Carthusian monks in their monasteries.

← I USED TO BE "THE LADY IN GRAY"

Now, I can be pretty much any color I like. There are even British shorthairs with three-color, tiger-striped, or spotted coats.

↑

MALAYAN

I love to meow, especially late at night. For some strange reason, my human roomies tend to be bothered by it.

MEOW NEWS

123rd YEAR — No. 1474 🐾 SINCE 1892 🐾 WEDNESDAY, OCTOBER 7, 2015 🐾 PRICE: 25 CAT HAIRS

THE CHESHiRE CAT AND HiS MYSTERiOUS SMiLE

Drawing a mysterious cat with a huge grin isn't exactly a walk in the park. Just ask the man who drew the Cheshire cat, first introduced in the children's book *Alice in Wonderland*!

It's getting dark. The clock is striking five—time to enjoy a refreshing cup of tea! John Tenniel, an illustrator,

is sitting in his room, deep in thought. His friend, the writer Lewis Carroll, asked him to draw a cat for his book, *Alice in Wonderland*. "I'm too bad of a draftsman to do it myself," Carroll said. "I need a professional to do it." That's because he didn't want just any ordinary cat. Carroll himself had tried to draw his mysterious smile, but it resulted only in a bin of wasted paper.

Tenniel takes a sip of the tea, and a mischievous smile lights up his face—he's got an idea. That gray cat on the wrapper of the cheese he had for breakfast came to mind . . . And the British shorthair from a week ago, the one who destroyed his kitchen tablecloth with her muddy paws . . . He caught her right in the act, but she smiled at him as if nothing had happened. Or those grimacing cat heads he's been seeing on church walls since childhood. "My beautiful muses!" he rejoices and dips the tip of his pen into an ink well, not stopping until his table is sagging under the weight of the 92 total illustrations, one of them a drawing of the Cheshire cat with a dazzling guilty smile. Tenniel doesn't know it yet, but he's just made one of the most famous illustrations in modern history.

A funny detail: Did you know that a group of distant galaxies bears the name of the Cheshire cat? That's because just like in Carroll's story, these galaxies appear in your telescope and then vanish like a cloud of steam, meaning that scientists still aren't sure if they actually exist.

~ Paws, editor ~

SCOTTISH FOLD

I'm said to resemble an owl due to my short, sort of folded ears and wise eyes. What do you think? Hoot, hoot . . . ahem, actually, meow!

OWL AMONG CATS

APPEARANCE

ROUND HEAD AND WIDE EYES THAT HAVE A SWEET INNOCENT LOOK

YOU CAN RECOGNIZE ME BY MY FOLDED EARS (THOUGH THEY LOOKED COMPLETELY NORMAL WHEN I WAS BORN)

I CAN BE LONGHAIRED OR SHORTHAIRED

I HAVE SOMEWHAT SHORT LEGS

HOW I SAW THE LIGHT OF DAY

The first known Scottish fold was my great-great-great grandmother Susie, who lived a happy feline life at a farm in the Scottish county of Perthshire. In 1961, she got noticed by a neighbor, a cat breeder and enthusiast who was so captivated by Susie and her kittens that five years later he set up a breeding station for this breed.

THREE TYPES OF FOLDS

1. Single fold
2. Double fold
3. Triple fold

1. **2.** **3.**

THREE TYPES OF FOLDS ⬆

The era of our ear folds was kicked off by my great-great-great-grandmother Susie. But just to let you know, it isn't as simple as it may seem. Some of us have ears that are folded just a teensy little bit—simply put, their tips are the only thing that's tilted. The ears of others are folded straight in the middle. And some of my relatives have ears that are pressed close to their heads, making their adorable faces seem perfectly round.

⬆ TEMPERAMENT

Generally speaking, I'm a walking advertisement for feline happiness. I tend to be in a good mood and love my human family, children, and animal companions. I like to play, especially out in the wild, and will come asking to be pet every once in a while. But I have a mind of my own. I wouldn't be a cat if I didn't, would I? And don't leave me alone for too long, I hate that! Spit, scratch!

LIKE BUDDHA ➡

I've discovered the secret of divine comfort! Simply squat, straighten up, stretch your hind legs forward, and place the front ones on your tummy. People say I look like the Buddha when sitting like that.

← JUST LET ME SLEEP

Ah, I really need to stretch and have a rest . . . I could spend the whole day lying around, no problem. And I'm not alone! We, the Scottish folds, are, shall we say, a little bit lazy—every single one of us. It's in our genes. We're so lazy that we don't even feel like purring. Purring makes one tired . . . and let's not even mention walking! We love it when humans carry us from one place to another, or when we can watch a TV show with you. Those of you who can't fall asleep when someone's snoring nearby—better stock up on earplugs because oh boy, do we ever snore. That's right! We lie back, close our eyes, and . . . zzzzzzzz, zzzzzzzz . . .

CHERCHEZ LA GÈNES

Shortly after Susie was discovered, scientists started investigating our unusual folds. They learned it was caused by a gene that's passed down to all of the breed's kittens, though it manifests only in some of them. One of my brothers, for example, has folded ears, while the other has retained long straight ears into adulthood.

SCOTTISH FOLD COLOR VARIETIES

1. White
2. Tortoiseshell
3. Gray
4. Tri Color (Calico)
5. Cream
6. Golden Chinchilla

1. 2. 3. 4. 5. 6.

MEOW NEWS

127th YEAR — No. 1521 🐾 SINCE 1892 🐾 TUESDAY, SEPTEMBER 24, 2019 🐾 PRICE: 25 CAT HAIRS

CATS AND THEIR INNER BEAUTY

Dear human readers, this story is mainly for you. Since the last edition was published, we've been flooded with hundreds of angry letters, sent by your own kitties.

Even our editorial team was moved to tears by the courage of Calippo, a Scottish fold who shared her life story. "You know, as a cat owned by a famous singer, I have everything my humble kitty heart could desire," she confided in us. "Except good health. I might look adorable, and sure, it makes me happy to hear others say so, but it also comes with many health issues. Jumping is harder for me, and forget about whipping my tail as briskly as other cats. If I had a choice, I would have been born an ordinary kitten," Calippo admits and adds, hoping that her

owner will read her plea, "I hope to marry a regular abandoned tabby from the streets someday! That would make me hopeful that my kittens would be able to leap around, jump, and frolic with no reservations. I don't care about appearances; I'm sure he'll captivate me with his inner beauty," she concludes confidently, and we can only agree.

Well, our thoughtful cat lovers of all stripes—go ahead and rescue an abandoned cat or kittent! They'll thank you for your generosity in their own cat way! Or if you can't do that, at least bring some good food to the shelter so that they, too, can spend their Christmas feasting like the kings and queens they are!

Blue-Eyes, editor-in-chief,
a happy rescue from a waste bin

AMERiCAN CURL

I may look like an alien with a pair of antennas on my head, but believe you me—I'm a flesh-and-blood cat and my feet are planted firmly on the ground.

INTELLIGENCE: 🐾🐾🐾🐾🐾

STUBBORNNESS: In the end, you can always talk me around.

ACTIVITY LEVEL: Romper

INCLINED TO RUN AWAY: 🐾🐾

CUDDLY: 🐾🐾🐾🐾🐾

A LOYAL FAMILY FRIEND

TEMPERAMENT

I love my family, and most of all the young humans—those are my real partners in crime. I may not be chatty, but I more than make up for it with playing and romping. *Hop!* I bet you can't catch me! Meow! If children aren't around, I can do just fine with adults—I enjoy watching them do whatever they do.

APPEARANCE

I BOAST WIDE EARS WITH CURLED TIPS THAT CAN DO A 180-DEGREE TURN

I HAVE A SMOOTH COAT WITH AN UNDERCOAT, FITTING CLOSELY TO THE BODY

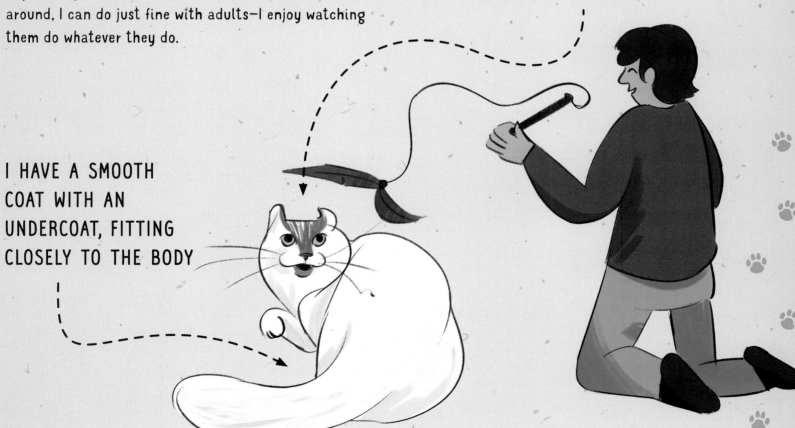

HOW i SAW THE LiGHT OF DAY

A stray kitten was found in 1981 in California. It would have ended up like millions of its predecessors, were it not for the two nice people it charmed, as only we, the American curls, can. The kitten's ears were curled backward, like a pair of devil's horns. Shulamith—that's what the new owners called this oddity—went on to become the foremother of our breed.

FRIENDLY, ALMOND-SHAPED EYES

AMERICAN CURL COLOR VARIETIES

1. Red tabby
2. Silver & white
3. White & black
4. Blue
5. White & golden
6. Tri Color (Calico)

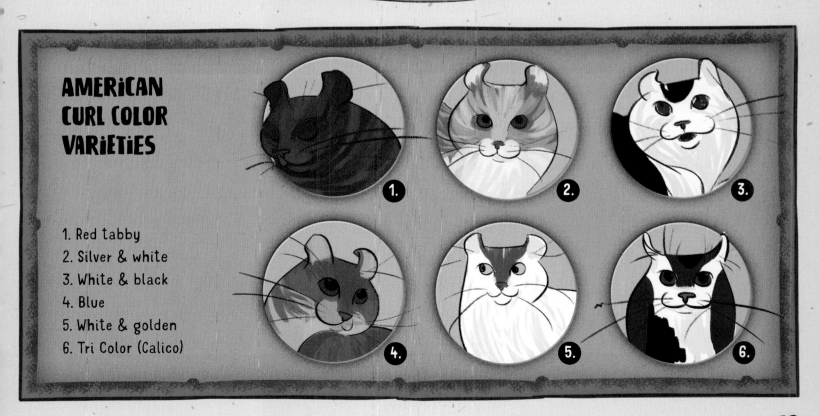

← DOMESTIC CAT — ENHANCED EDITION

Even though our foremother Shulamith passed down the gene that makes our ears all curled, we are the same relaxed, grateful, active, and sociable domestic cats we've always been. What I'm really grateful for is that this mostly keeps us healthy and free of the diseases from which some other cat breeds suffer. We can jump and frolic well into old age—Hop! Scratch! Crash! Leap!

THE MORE FRIENDS, THE BETTER

Some cats may enjoy their peace and quiet in a nice warm spot, but I don't. I don't mind if the house is bustling with many children and animals. Just make sure I'm always the center of attention.

MEOW NEWS

123rd YEAR — No. 1469   SINCE 1892   TUESDAY, MAY 26, 2015   PRICE: 25 CAT HAIRS

FREEWAY: MENACE TO THE ROADS

Cats are said to have nine lives. But sometimes, even we can find ourselves in a pickle—a tricky situation we don't know how to get out of. An American curl named Freeway could tell you all about it. Let's find out how he got his unusual name.

Freeway loves roads. And not just small dirt roads but wild highways with several lanes—or really, anywhere with heavy traffic and lots of noise! One day, though, his love for the hum of car engines backfired on him, so to speak. He went to a particularly dangerous highway, and yikes! "I was having so much fun, enjoying the whooshing—cars were hurtling in both directions. And then I noticed that I'd strayed too far. I became trapped and couldn't escape. All I could do

was crawl atop a thin steel fence that separated both lanes. I hung on and desperately meowed for help. Meooooow!" recalls Freeway, recounting his moment of terror.

"A few drivers saw me but none dared to stop. Until Richard appeared." "As soon as I noticed the kitty, I knew he needed my help. I pulled over and ran to get him. He was giving me this pleading look with his wide amber eyes. Before I knew it, he was in my arms, purring with delight and relief," says Richard, who ended up adopting the restless tomcat and believes anyone would have done what he did. "We should all help each other, regardless of whether we're human, or covered in fur." Our editorial team can only agree.

MUNCHKIN

I'm a dream come true for anyone who loves Dachshunds. Don't mistake me for a dog, though—I'm a proud lady with a typically catlike temperament.

INTELLIGENCE: 🐾🐾🐾🐾🐾

STUBBORNNESS: 🐾🐾🐾🐾🐾🐾

PERSONALITY: Jet plane

WANDERLUST: I love to wander around the neighborhood, just like most domestic cats.

CUDDLINESS: 🐾🐾🐾🐾🐾

CAT DACHSHUND WITH A HEART OF GOLD

APPEARANCE

I CAN BE SHORTHAIRED OR LONGHAIRED. AT SHOWS, WE'RE JUDGED SEPARATELY

I'M OF A SMALLISH STATURE

I MAY LOOK LIKE AN ORDINARY DOMESTIC CAT, BUT MY DISTINCT SHORT LEGS SET ME APART

TEMPERAMENT

I may have short legs, but this takes nothing away from my confidence and pride. I'm independent, friendly to other animals and humans, and cuddly, and I can run or romp just like any other cat. The only thing that's different with me is that I most likely won't be jumping up onto your kitchen counter. No hard feelings, countertop—I just can't reach you. What a pity . . .

HOW i SAW THE LiGHT OF DAY

In 1983 in Louisiana, a music teacher rescued two short-legged pregnant cats. Apparently, some boneheaded bulldog chased them under a truck. Can you imagine? The lady named one of them Blackberry and kept her. Blackberry gave birth to several kittens, all with short legs. One of them was a tomcat named Toulouse who grew up to love running around the neighborhood. Thanks to his popularity among the feline ladies, short-legged cats soon set off around the world . . .

MUNCHKiN COLOR VARiETiES

1. Silver
2. Black & white
3. Blue tabby with white spots
4. Tri Color (Calico)
5. Cream
6. Tortoiseshell tabby

← THE CAT WIZARD OF OZ

We boast the unusual name "Munchkin" to honor the great American writer L. Frank Baum, who wrote many novels about a girl named Dorothy and the Wizard of Oz. These stories feature a group of skillful dwarves who are called Munchkins.

A CONTROVERSIAL "BREED" →

In 1994, I actually caused a longtime judge of a certain international cat association, one that determines which cat breeds are officially recognized, to resign in protest. The organization had recognized me as a new breed, but the judge believed that we Munchkins would suffer from painful arthritis, deformed spines and chests, and many other issues, and therefore didn't want people to keep breeding us. But even though groups like the Humane Society of the United States are right when they say it's bad to breed animals for exaggerated body parts when it harms our health and well-being, some of us Munchkins do live long, healthy, and perfectly happy lives.

HOW COULD ANYONE GET US MIXED UP?

← MINUET (NAPOLEON CAT)

As another unrecognized breed, I came to be as a result of the difficult cross-breeding between a Munchkin cat and a Persian cat. Why am I called Napoleon, you ask? After the infamous French commander, of course—the one who was so famously short!

MEOW NEWS

127th YEAR — No. 1524 🐾 SINCE 1892 🐾 SUNDAY, DECEMBER 8, 2019 🐾 PRICE: 25 CAT HAIRS

SQUIRREL, OR A CAT?

Monday quiz

Dear cats and kittens—it's been about a week since our editorial team received the following photo. Take a good look at it ... And now guess: Does it show a cat, or a squirrel? What do you think? A round little face, short legs, a shaggy tail ... Do you have your answer ready?

... We won't keep you in suspense any longer. Our editorial team spent a whole week looking for this mysterious creature. And after an exhausting search, we actually succeeded! The creature's name is Bell and it's an adorable cat of the Napoleon breed, living in Japan with her one cat sibling. Bell revealed that she loves

food, can stand on her hind legs, and utterly adores wearing lace collars! But when we dared to ask her how tall she was, she answered as forcefully as the world-renowned military leader (Napoleon, 5.5 feet) whose name her family bears.

"If you make fun of my height," she warned, "I'll jump on you and lie on top of you, grrr!" (Note: It really did sound like growling, not like the standard purring that cats do.) This simply disarmed us. It was clear she'd gotten cuteness, the secret weapon of cats, down to a fine art and wasn't afraid to use it under any circumstances! ☺

MANX CAT

You mean to say you don't know of the Isle of Man? Jeez. Grab a globe, then, and find this tiny, inconspicuous corner of the world—that's where I come from. Just like the island, I too am unique, ancient, and mysterious, but also loyal, proud, and friendly toward humans. And what would you know—I don't have a tail! Still, I've enchanted many a cat owner.

WE'RE CAT ROYALTY

INTELLIGENCE: 🐾🐾🐾🐾🐾

STUBBORNNESS: 🐾🐾

PERSONALITY: Romper (but beware, mice!)

WANDERLUST: 🐾🐾🐾

CUDDLINESS: 🐾🐾🐾🐾

APPEARANCE

SOME OF US HAVE A HINT OF A TAIL, OR EVEN A SHORT STUMP, BUT HAVING NO TAIL AT ALL IS THE MOST COMMON FOR OUR BREED - - -

I HAVE A BODY WITH NO FLAB

TEMPERAMENT

I may lack a tail, but I definitely don't lack the qualities that make an ideal cat companion: I'm calm and even-tempered, cuddly with my humans, and wary of those I don't know. You might be surprised to learn how smart I am—I can even learn to fetch!

I HAVE A ROUND HEAD WITH POINTY EARS AND A DISTINCT NOSE - - -

MY HIND LEGS ARE LONGER THAN THE FORELEGS, WHICH MAKES ME LOOK LIKE A RABBIT WHEN I'M RUNNING

HOW COULD ANYONE GET US MIXED UP?

PiXiE BOB

What do I remind you of? Hopefully, you've guessed correctly and answered "bobcat."

AMERICAN BOBTAiL ➡

They call me "the golden retriever of cats" because my temperament resembles that of a dog and I'm very easy to train.

KURiLiAN BOBTAiL

My wild ancestors lost their long tails over time because they tended to freeze solid in the harsh wilderness of the Russian Far East—not too fun, let me tell you.

⬅ JAPANESE BOBTAiL

I remember the era of the heroic samurai and noble geisha. My tail can be over four inches long, but it seems shorter because it's crooked.

HOW I SAW THE LIGHT OF DAY ⟸

No one knows when exactly, but one day a tailless kitten was born on the Isle of Man. Humans and other cats were completely flabbergasted by it! When it became an adult, its admired peculiarity was passed down to all of the original cat's kittens and then to their kittens, and then their kittens ... you get the idea. We pretty much conquered the whole island. Nowadays, when anyone living on the Isle of Man happens to spot a cat with a tail, they point their fingers at the strange creature and marvel.

EVERYONE WANTS ME ➡

In the 19th century, my unusual appearance caught the eye of Edward VII, a British king who went on to keep several Manx cats. My popularity skyrocketed so much that there was a real danger of people taking away all tailless cats from the Isle of Man, thereby causing my breed to die out. So, the government established a national breeding station, helping tailless Manx cats survive. The people from the Isle of Man respect me a great deal, and they even made me their national symbol.

OTHER CATS WITH A SHORT TAIL

1. American Bobtail
2. Pixie Bob
3. Kurilian Bobtail
4. Japanese Bobtail
5. Cymric Cat

MEOW NEWS

123rd YEAR — No. 1472 🐾 SINCE 1892 🐾 SUNDAY, AUGUST 2, 2015 🐾 PRICE: 25 CAT HAIRS

As you probably know, the world has no shortage of cats. Sometimes, there's way too many of us, and kind generous souls willing to care for abandoned kitties are rare. And if you'd like for those kind souls to be gorilla souls, then you're truly out of luck! But wouldn't you know it? There actually is one such benevolent primate out there.

Her name is Koko and she's quite the rarity. Her maternal instinct manifested itself as early as Christmas 1983, when she wanted a kitty as a present. Psychologist Francine Patterson, her caretaker, didn't take her seriously at first and got her an ordinary stuffed toy. But Koko immediately let her know that no toy could ever replace a living kitten. And so when her birthday came on July 4, 1984, she was allowed to pick an abandoned kitten from a rescue shelter. Koko gently stroked the tiny gray ball of fur and named him All Ball. From then on, she treated him like a baby gorilla. And maybe she even tried to teach him sign language—all 1,000 signs she knows!

KOKO THE GORiLLA HAS A KiTTEN! SHE NAMES HiM "ALL BALL"

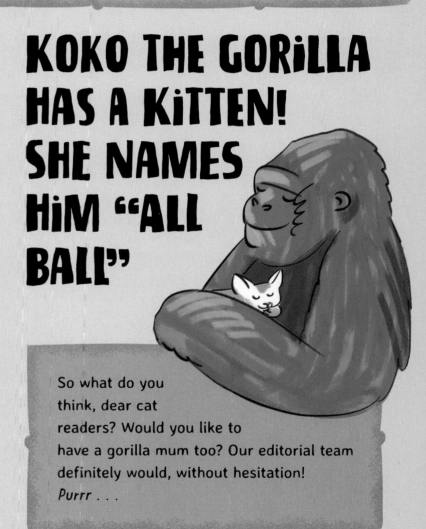

So what do you think, dear cat readers? Would you like to have a gorilla mum too? Our editorial team definitely would, without hesitation! *Purrr . . .*

KOKO'S STORY CONTiNUES: TOMORROW iS ANOTHER DAY

Koko, a western lowland gorilla who raised All Ball, a kitten she later tragically lost, hasn't stopped loving Manx cats. Over time, the meowing of four new little scamps has filled her life: Miss Black, Miss Gray, Lipstick, and Smoky.

PERSiAN CAT

People apparently can't agree whether my long shaggy coat and flat nose are a mark of nobility and perfection, or if they're a nightmare made flesh. Hey! I love myself just the way I am.

INTELLIGENCE: 🐾🐾

STUBBORNNESS: 🐾🐾🐾🐾🐾

PERSONALITY: Diehard couching enthusiast. (You'll never get me off the couch!)

WANDERLUST: 🐾

CUDDLINESS: 🐾🐾

YOU EiTHER LOVE HER, OR HATE HER

TEMPERAMENT

A "couch cat"—that's not an insult but high praise to me. After all, there's nothing better than taking a nap on a comfortable pillow before the main duties of the day commence—proper lounging, of course! I'm very mild-mannered and quiet and will happily serve as a warm ornament in your apartment. Some might call me lazy but don't believe them. I simply have a preferred lifestyle. My beloved humans feed me, pet me, brush my long coat, and I . . . well, sometimes I don't even notice when they're away for the weekend.

MEDIUM-SIZED BODY THAT LOOKS MUCH LARGER DUE TO THE LONG THICK COAT

APPEARANCE

ROUND HEAD WITH A DISTINCT FLAT NOSE AND WIDE JAWS

HUGE ROUND EYES THAT ARE EITHER ORANGE, GREEN, OR BLUE - - - -

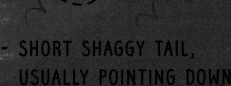

SHORT SHAGGY TAIL, USUALLY POINTING DOWN

HOW i SAW THE LiGHT OF DAY

Rumor has it that ages ago, my ancestors lived in Persia, in modern-day Iraq. In the 16th century, the Italian nobleman Pietro della Valle fell in love with me while traveling around the Middle East and brought as many as eight kittens back home to Europe. Surrounded by common European cats, those longhair bundles must have seemed as if they were from a whole different world! No wonder, then, that we eventually came to America and then reached all of the continents on the planet inhabited by humans.

SiLKY COAT THAT ⬅ REQUiRES REGULAR CARE

Many people are deterred from getting a Persian kitten by the idea that taking care of my coat is some horrible chore. Yes, I need to be brushed every single day, but in doing so, you'll be rewarded with a silky plump coat that will always cheer you up. And I enjoy brushing the same way humans enjoy massages . . . Yawn!

PERSIAN CAT COLOR VARIETIES

1. White
2. Brown tabby
3. Black
4. Tortoiseshell
5. Red & white
6. Silver spotted blue tabby

← NO, WE REALLY DIDN'T SMASH INTO THE WALL FACE FIRST WHEN WE WERE KITTENS!

All Persian cats must have this distinct flat nose ... or not? Believe it or not, up until the mid-20th century, the faces of my ancestors were longer than mine. A few kittens with the then unusual flat face were born. Breeders found them so cute they decided to keep this surprising characteristic in the Persian breed. Long-nosed Persian cats, however, are still around today.

i WON THE FIRST EVER CAT SHOW! ➜

It took place in 1871 in London and was a huge hit—about 20,000 visitors came to see the cats on display! Competing with many breeds that were well known back then, such as the Siamese, Angora, Scottish wildcat, and many others, I nevertheless stole the show and went home with the gold.

I. DON'T. LIKE. YOU. MEET THE WORLD'S GRUMPIEST CAT!

Shake paws with Garfi, the grumpiest cat on the planet. Or better yet don't ... Sometimes it's wise not to take unnecessary risks. Who knows if he'd like you. Probably not. He'll definitely spend the entire day looking like he hates you, until you start believing it. Mimi and Kri, our experts in feline facial expressions who search for missing cats in their spare time and work with leading feline detectives and criminologists, formulated three hypotheses to explain why Garfi looks like such a killjoy:

1) Garfi hasn't slept well.

2) There's something Garfi really doesn't like (and he doesn't try to hide his distaste).

3) Garfi is actually the happiest cat around but is deeply worried that he wouldn't look good if he wore a wide grin or that his owner and other cats wouldn't pay him his due respect. That's why he's hiding his true feeling underneath the mask of a heartless tomcat others need to be wary of.

The surprising truth was revealed to Mimi and Kri by Garfi's human Hulya Ozkok in Turkey: "I know he looks ready to get his claws out at any moment ... But he's a sweetheart, truly!" she raves emotionally. As she says this, Garfi is sitting on her lap, enjoying a good petting behind his ears and purring contentedly. Believe it or not, he really does seem happy after all!

Curiosities of the cat world

Give him a fresh turkey roast and his face will say: No.

Give him a warm bath: I don't like you.

Read him a bedtime story: Have I ever told you that I don't like you?

Give him a hat to keep him warm while he frolics in the snow: I. Will. Bite. You!

EXOTIC CAT

Close your eyes and think of a soft teddy bear you can lovingly cuddle . . . And now imagine that the teddy bear comes alive in your arms, purring contentedly. That's me! *Purrrrr.*

INTELLIGENCE: 🐾🐾🐾🐾🐾

STUBBORNNESS: 🐾

PERSONALITY: Couch potato (What? I need my beauty sleep!)

WANDERLUST: 🐾

CUDDLINESS: One of the cuddliest there is!

YOUR SOFT PURRING BALL OF HAPPINESS

APPEARANCE

LARGE, UNUSUALLY ROUND HEAD WITH WIDE CHEEKS & SHORT NOSE THAT SOMETIMES MAKES IT DIFFICULT TO BREATHE

MIDSIZED, MUSCLED, ROUND-SHAPED BODY, THICK COAT WITH AN UNDERCOAT

TEMPERAMENT

You'd be hard-pressed to find a calmer, more peaceful companion than me. I don't mind just lying around all day, not doing anything important. (After all, my humans are there to get me food, aren't they?) But I am pretty curious and keep an eye on my human and animal buddies, whom I can come to love very deeply.

Unlike most other cat breeds, I age very slowly, meaning that I enter puberty at a later age and become an adult as late as two years after birth. Regardless, I love cuddling and snuggling my entire life.

LITTLE NOSE, BIG TROUBLES →

The Persian cat left me her short nose, which makes it hard for me to breathe whenever I have the bad idea of exercising . . . Often, it also blocks my tear ducts. That's why my human must clean my eyes daily, using a wet swab.

EXOTIC CAT COLOR VARIETIES

1. Ginger & white
2. White
3. Gray
4. Gray & white
5. Tri color (Calico)
6. Fawn & white

CAN i HOP iN WiTH YOU?

I'm a typical example of a couch cat. While other cats might be tempted to frolic in the garden to their heart's content, I enjoy being at home, lying in my human's bed. And hey, it wouldn't do for a couch cat to catch a cold, would it?

HOW i SAW THE LiGHT OF DAY

In the 1960s, American breeders started wondering what the Persian cat would look like if it was a shorthair. So they began breeding the Persian cat with the American shorthair cat, and voilà—come 1966, I was officially recognized as a separate breed. But still, me and the Persian are basically joined at the hip: I inherited her temperament, appearance, everything.

GARFIELD   Monday quiz

The best known exotic cat is probably Garfield, who was created by Jim Davis in 1978. Who hasn't heard of him, you say? But do you really know him? Rack your cat brains and find out in our test:

1) What's Garfield's favorite meal?
a) broccoli, b) lasagna, c) both

2) Which day of the week does Garfield hate the most?
a) Sunday because he must wake up early to catch all the mice he'll be eating the next week (so that he can idle the rest of the week away), b) Monday (he's unhappy that Jon must go to work again, but is too proud to actually say so), c) Wednesday because the weekend is still too far away.

3) Do you know the names of Garfield's fellow animal friends?
a) Odie and Nermal, b) Jon and Liz, c) Otylia and Serval

4) Where was Garfield born?
a) Right in the middle of an Italian restaurant, b) In the head of cartoonist Jim Davis, c) Both are correct

5) And finally, one trick question: What breed is Garfield?
a) He's an exotic cat, naturally, b) He's a ginger crossbreed, fat and lazy, but sort of looks like an exotic cat (his outrageously pampered temperament seems to have been passed down to him), c) I think he's an American shorthair

Add 1 canary for each correct answer: 1b, 2b, 3a, 4c, 5b
5 canaries: Is your name Garfield by any chance? You know him so well you two might be twins.
3-4 canaries: Not so bad. You definitely scored higher than Mondays. ☺
0-2 canaries: Maybe you should stop lazing about on the couch so much—or at least do it with a comic strip in hand! ☺

MAINE COON

You now have the honor of meeting the largest cat in the world! It's quite common for our males to weigh as much as a child that's 18 months old—which is a plus, since we love to play with children.

GENTLE GIANT

INTELLIGENCE: 🐾🐾🐾🐾🐾

STUBBORNNESS: 🐾🐾🐾

PERSONALITY: Cool bird (enthusiastic play doesn't necessarily equal running like a maniac)

WANDERLUST: 🐾🐾

CUDDLINESS: 🐾🐾🐾🐾🐾🐾

APPEARANCE

HIGH CHEEKBONES AND A DISTINCT NOSE

LARGE, STRONG, ANGULAR BODY WITH A LONGISH COAT THAT NEEDS REGULAR COMBING

LONG SHAGGY TAIL THAT RESEMBLES THAT OF A RACCOON

TEMPERAMENT

I'm a family darling. That's because I love kids and am playful as well as cuddly. But at the same time—and I'm proud of this!—I don't impose on my humans. When they're not home, I find my own entertainment. Why spend my time wallowing? Especially when I can take a great long nap in the meantime. I can fall asleep pretty much anywhere in any position, regardless of how uncomfortable it is—upside down, wrapped around the leg of an armchair, crammed in a dollhouse... Why should I deny myself a bit of luxurious sleep just because I'm not currently lying on a pillow...

WHILE FEMALES WEIGH "ONLY" 10 TO 15 POUNDS, MALES USUALLY WEIGH IN AT ANYWHERE FROM 20 TO 25 POUNDS!

WATER ONLY FROM A BOWL

When people see me drink water, they laugh for some reason. Probably because I first pat the surface a couple of times to chase away the cat staring at me from the bowl. Only then do I take a sip. Sometimes, I ladle up the water with my paw. You should try it yourself—it's really practical, *meow!*

HOW i SAW THE LiGHT OF DAY

No one knows exactly how I came to be. What is known is that I'm a crossbreed between the American shorthair and the Norwegian Forest cat. So who, then, brought my European ancestor to the US, you ask? It's rumored to have been Charles Coon, a British seafarer, or even Marie Antoinette, who had the cat transported to America. Either way, people first noticed us in the 19th century up in Maine, on the East Coast. Back then, we were still catching mice and didn't do too much of that good old lying around on people's couches.

QUiET MEOWiNG, LOUD PURRiNG

I don't need to yell like crazy. To communicate, all I need is a soft gentle meow. Purring, though, that's another story. I purr deeply and loudly. It sounds like a dove cooing, just to let you know I'm having a great time with you. Coo, ahem, *purrrr!*

MEOW NEWS

99th YEAR — No. 1183 SINCE 1892 SUNDAY, JULY 21, 1991 PRICE: 25 CAT HAIRS

THE OLD MAN AND THE KiTTEN

Bedtime stories

Winter has come, dear kittens, and a wondrous fairy tale has come with it! So snuggle up in your beds and perk up your ears. Can you hear the crackling of logs in the fireplace? Pour yourselves a bowl of nice warm cat milk and paw through today's Christmas story.

Once upon a time, there was a bearded writer named Ernest Hemingway—a giant of a man with a deep voice he rarely used. A lot of people viewed him as an oddball because of it.

One day in his favorite bar, Sloppy Joe's in Key West, Florida, he met an old friend—a ship captain named Stanley Dexter. "You can't be a loner forever," Stanley said all of a sudden. "You could use some company.

 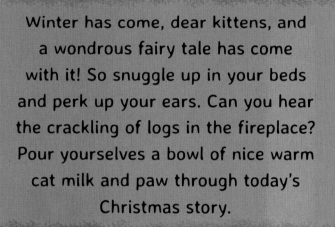

Here," he added and gave Hemingway his ship's cat, Snow White. She was no ordinary cat. She was a seafaring cat who had cruised the seas with Stanley. And to make sure Snow White wouldn't slip on the deck whenever a cold wave crashed into the ship, she was born with six toes on each paw. Regular cats have only five toes on the front paws and four toes on the hind paws. The writer hesitated, but in the end accepted this odd gift.

The people in his life claimed that from then on, Snow White helped the old man with his writing, He became a new person, a lovey-dovey one, and he even considered another feline addition. Privately, he wrote in his journal,

"A cat has absolute emotional honesty: human beings, for one reason or another, may hide their feelings, but a cat does not."

Hemingway's love of six-toed kitties, mostly Maine coons, was so strong that in the end his house resounded with the meowing of not one but fifty more cats. When his friends dared suggest he might be overdoing it, he smiled and remarked, "Well, you know, one cat just leads to another."

NORWEGIAN FOREST CAT

I'm an adorable shag of hair who doesn't lounge around on the couch but instead hunts for mice or birds if given the opportunity. I was bred to perfection by the Scandinavian wilderness, where my wild relatives still live.

A ROBUST YET GENTLE NORTHERN BEAUTY

TEMPERAMENT

I'm calm and friendly, but not lazy in the least. I love sharing my home with other cats, dogs, or (worst-case scenario) some silly hamster, if you absolutely insist ... Don't let my robust stature frighten you—I really won't even think about scratching or biting you (unless you decide to pull my tail, are we clear?). But I need to have enough space to do my climbing and frolicking—a tiny flat with no jungle gym and scratching post sounds anything but fun to me, *meow, meow.* I'm also partial to children, like you—we'll be excellent friends!

THICK WATERPROOF COAT – –

SHAGGY TAIL

UNLIKE OTHER BREEDS WITH LONGISH COATS, I SEEM SLENDER. THAT'S BECAUSE MY LEGS AND BODY ARE LONG

APPEARANCE

UNLIKE SHORTHAIR CATS, I HAVE HAIRS GROWING BETWEEN MY PAW PADS (WHICH IS INVALUABLE - - IN SNOW!)

TRIANGULAR HEAD WITH LONG EARS

← HOW I SAW THE LIGHT OF DAY

I'm from Scandinavia, where I've long lived in the peaceful wilderness—that's why I'm perfectly adapted to the long, cruel, wet winters and the hot arid summers that are typical for Norway, my homeland. No one knows where and how I appeared exactly, but I may have descended from wild shorthairs mating with Persian cats, transported by Scandinavian sailors long ago. We've hunted mice on farms for many generations, but only in the 1930s did people start keeping us on purpose.

COAT FOR ANY SEASON →

Would you believe that not only people but also we Norwegian Forest cats change coats depending on the season? In winter, we grow a very warm coat with a thick underfur that protects us against bitter cold. In summer, though, we get a thin underfur so that we won't sweat too much. Your puny central heating or air conditioning can't hold a candle to us!

NORWEGIAN FOREST CAT COLOR VARIETIES

1. Brown tabby & white
2. White
3. Blue tabby
4. Black
5. Red & white
6. Tri Color (Calico)

HOW COULD ANYONE GET US MIXED UP?

← NEBELUNG

I look like the Russian blue. In fact, I'm her longhair version. I'm somewhat shy and guarded, but if you win me over I'll love you forever.

RAGAMUFFIN ➡

I'm very calm and friendly and love being pampered. For example, you should brush me at least once a week. I'm closely related to the ragdoll breed.

← SIBERIAN CAT

I may come from the northern wilds of Siberia, but I am very friendly and cuddly. I tend to be very dependent on my human pack. What? You dare leave without me? All the way over to . . . the next room?!

MEOW NEWS

98th YEAR — No. 1172 🐾 SINCE 1892 🐾 FRIDAY, AUGUST 31, 1990 🐾 PRICE: 25 CAT HAIRS

DEWEY READMORE BOOKS iNViTES YOU TO A LiBRARY

Dear bookworm cats, fans of *Meow News*, and anything that can be read, I'd hereby like to invite you to visit my library in the town of Spencer, Iowa.

You may be wondering what this tomcat with such a shaggy coat—perhaps passed down to him by his ancestors who lived deep in the woods of Norway—is doing in the middle of a room filled with strange letters. Well, listen to my story.

One chilly night in January, when I was a mere eight-week-old kitten, I woke up all of a sudden, sitting in an book crate. I had no idea how this happened. I meowed my tiny kitten lungs out, but no one came to help me. I didn't get warm until morning, when a librarian named Vicky took me and a couple of books out of the box. Rescue had arrived! Vicky looked at me in surprise. The ice crystals in my whiskers began thawing, but I was still trembling all over. Vicky wrapped me in a warm towel and brought me inside the library, where I immediately curled up below a radiator. It was so quiet

and warm . . . I loved it there. But would I be allowed to stay forever? Vicky gave me a name, Dewey Readmore Books, so it seemed that my mission was clear. But the library board and the town's mayor needed some convincing. I was a little bit nervous when I introduced myself, determined to use the best weapon cats have at our disposal—rubbing against their legs and purring appealingly. In the end, we shook paws and I left with a discount coupon so that I could see a vet. Since then, I've been a full-time librarian.

I began meowing to people about books, until more and more visitors started coming! Then they began talking to one another. For a short while, I even became a cat writer. (Vicky had to transcribe my stories into her human language, saying that people wouldn't be able to read my paw prints.)

So here's my invitation—come read with us! Maybe we'll get to meet each other.

SNOWSHOE

I'm kind of a hodgepodge of different cats: my white paws, passed down to me by my ancestors, have walked in both cute American courtyards and ancient Thai temples.

INTELLIGENCE: 🐾🐾🐾🐾🐾
STUBBORNNESS: 🐾🐾🐾
PERSONALITY: Companionship addict (I can be at home without you only if you find me some animal buddies.)
WANDERLUST: 🐾🐾
CUDDLINESS: 🐾🐾🐾🐾🐾🐾

CHATTY CUDDLEBUG iN WHiTE SOCKS

TEMPERAMENT

I'm a sensitive kitty who treasures her peace and quiet. But if you provide me with enough love and safety, I can discover my curious side and sense of adventure. I always need a pair of loving human arms to return to, though. Just like the Siamese cat, I too am sociable and will talk to you for as long as you're willing to listen. But unlike the Siamese, I don't shout—I'm a discreet talker. *Meow, meow, meow, meow, meow* . . .

BLUE EYES ONLY

ALL FOUR
PAWS ARE
SNOW-WHITE

APPEARANCE

LONGISH BODY BOASTING A COAT
WITH THE SAME CHARACTERISTICS
AS THAT OF A SIAMESE CAT

HOW i SAW THE LiGHT OF DAY

In the 1960s, when a favorite Siamese cat owned by the American breeder Dorothy Hinds-Daugherty unexpectedly gave birth to kittens with funny white paws (noticeably resembling those of the neighborhood Casanova!), no one had any idea the new mom had just entered into the annals of cat history. Dorothy fell in love with the kittens and began crossbreeding Siamese cats with the American shorthair. The resulting kittens, whose feet were white and whose bodies were the same color as that of a Siamese cat, were named Snowshoe cats. Sure, I could probably live with a more dignified name. But I forgive you, dear Dorothy—that's how magnanimous I am.

SECRET iN WHiTE ➡

Although our breed has existed for more than fifty years, I'm still a bit of a rarity. Anyone who wants to take me home needs to save quite a lot of money first. That's because we are all born completely white and it takes a few weeks before it's revealed which of the newborn kittens are Snowshoes and which aren't. Since we've inherited the genes of both the Siamese cat and the American shorthair, it's far from certain that a Snowshoe mom and a snowshoe dad will bring more Snowshoes into the world

It's said—and for good reason—that I'm very good-natured. I can tell when my owner is bothered by something, and try to make them happier, whatever it takes.

HAPPINESS IN A BALL

I can't deny my resemblance to the Siamese cat. That's why some people believe that I bring luck wherever my white paws go. Can I come share it with you too? *Meow, purrr...*

SNOWSHOE COLOR VARIETIES

1. Blue mask
2. Seal mask
3. Lilac mask
4. Traditional chocolate mask
5. Smaller and lighter chocolate mask
6. Chocolate mask & dark brown coat

MEOW NEWS

119th YEAR — No. 1419 ❧ SINCE 1892 ❧ SATURDAY, MARCH 5, 2011 ❧ PRICE: 25 CAT HAIRS

DUSTY, THE MOST ADORABLE THiEF iN THE WORLD

Caught
In The Act

A hidden camera captured an offender who'd committed a string of night burglaries in the city of San Mateo, California— an adorable Snowshoe tomcat whose thieving antics earned him the nickname Dusty the Klepto Kitty.

His turf? The neighborhood houses and gardens where he stashed an impressive 600 objects! So far, Dusty has declined every opportunity to explain his actions. When asked what motivated his crimes, he answered simply, "What if all that stuff comes in handy one day?" But Jean Chu, his human, showed us a complete list of the things he stole. Dusty's loot contains 16 car-washing gloves, 7 dish sponges, 213 dish towels, 7 rags, 5 towels, 18 shoes, 73 socks, 100 winter gloves, 1 pair of mittens, 3 aprons, 40 balls, 4 sets of underwear, 1 dog collar, 6 rubber ducks, 1 bed sheet, 3 leg warmers, 2 Frisbees, 1 golf cap, 1 surgical mask, 2 shopping bags, 1 bag of water balloons, 1 pair of pajama bottoms, 8 swimsuit pieces, and many, many more super-random items . . .

"Dusty can bring up to 11 things in one go. He likes to boast of his catch," Jean revealed. The little troublemaker is lucky that his robbed neighbors have no intention of putting him behind bars. "He's the cutest thief in the world," they say. "We don't call the police. We forgive him for everything. Secretly, we believe that his goal is to help clean our gardens from any clutter that has no place there."

Our editorial team just cracks up and wonders—whose house will Dusty clean next?

BiRMAN

Dong! Proud and noble, I squeeze past the temple gong and happily disappear into the arms of a bald monk . . . Or maybe it isn't a gong but the leg of your armchair? Well, OK, I will graciously allow you to scratch me behind the ear.

INTELLIGENCE: 🐾🐾🐾🐾
STUBBORNNESS: 🐾🐾🐾🐾
PERSONALITY: Cool bird (After all, I learned at the feet of Buddhist monks.)
WANDERLUST: 🐾🐾🐾
CUDDLINESS: 🐾🐾🐾🐾🐾🐾

A BLUE-EYED MONK iN WHiTE SOCKS

APPEARANCE

MALES ARE MUCH LARGER THAN FEMALES --

WIDE, ROUND HEAD WITH SKY-BLUE EYES (THAT YOU WON'T BE ABLE TO LOOK AWAY FROM)

SHORTISH YET MUSCLED LEGS, A STOCKY BODY ---

LIGHT, SEMI-LONG COAT WITH DARK MARKS ON THE FACE, EARS, LEGS, AND TAIL, BUT THE PAWS MUST ALWAYS BE WHITE!

HOW i SAW THE LIGHT OF DAY

Once upon a time, I used to live in the Buddhist temples of northern Burma, where they treated me like a goddess. Meow, those were the days . . . I was first recognized as a separate breed in 1925 in France, where I had arrived a few years earlier. But you know how things go . . . My time in the European sunlight didn't last long. World War II broke out and there were only two of us left on the entire continent! What saved us was breeding with Siamese and Persian cats. Thanks for the help, guys!

BALiNESE CAT

Meow, I'm a cuddly Siamese with a longhair coat. My name refers to my graceful movements, which resemble those of traditional Balinese dancers.

TEMPERAMENT

If you think a proud cat can't be good-natured, you've never met me. I don't like to brag, since modesty is my middle name, but even I must admit that people adore me because I'm kind and friendly. I feel very comfortable in your company, but don't feel the need to follow your every move—what am I, a dog? Boo! No, woof . . . meow!

HOW COULD ANYONE GET US MIXED UP?

HiMALAYAN CAT

I'm the ideal pet for people who don't spend a lot of time at home—I can manage on my own. Hiss!

RAGDOLL

Despite my name, I'm a wild giant. No toy factory could produce a creature with such a silky coat and such dazzling blue eyes as mine!

MEOW NEWS

123rd YEAR — No. 1468 ✸ SINCE 1892 ✸ TUESDAY, APRIL 14, 2015 ✸ PRICE: 25 CAT HAIRS

MADEMOiSELLE CHOUPETTE,
A FASHiON CELEBRiTY

Celebricats

Praline: Who would have thought that the great fashion guru Karl Lagerfeld would fall in love with a blue-eyed beauty, one with not two but four legs?

Choupette: Karl says that my eyes are the color of the ocean, purrr ... And besides, someone has to watch over him when he's walking down the catwalk, wearing those trademark black glasses of his. I prevent him from stumbling and losing his stern, respected face, *purrr* ...

Dear fans of the Daily Cat!
We bring you an interview with the great muse of fashion designer Karl Lagerfeld—graceful Birman Choupette! The interview with both superstars was conducted by Praline, our editor.

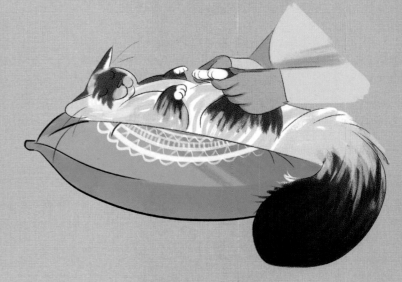

Praline: We wouldn't want that, for sure. Can you tell us how you two met?

Choupette: Our meeting was written in the stars, *meooow*... One day, my former servant and Karl's good friend left for a vacation. He wanted to take me with him, but I said that roaming around dusty roads like a vagrant would do my thick white coat no good. He listened and had Karl take care of me.

Lagerfeld: I would never have thought I'd take to an animal so much. (Unexpectedly, his powdered face turns red—ed. note.) As soon as my friend came back, I told him, "Too bad, mate. Choupette's mine, now!"

Praline: What's it like, Choupette, to live with a famous designer?

Choupette: I have everything a proper cat lady might need—two maids who take care of me 24/7. Sometimes, I meow politely to remind them I can actually do my own grooming. But on the other hand, who'd say no to some professional help! My coat is brushed by the softest brush six times a day, my belly is stroked for hours, and my paws are massaged. I also have my own chef who makes the choicest meaty delicacies for me every single day (I prefer prawns) and a muscled bodyguard who protects me from the lecherous eyes of stray tomcats. Karl says that I'm his muse—he's made hundreds of sketches of T-shirts and sweatshirts that bear my face! My eyes and groomed coat even graced the front page of both the human and cat *Vogue*. I'm also featured in a car commercial. What more could a cat princess want?

TURKiSH ANGORA

I'm one of the oldest breeds in the world. My friendly, loving nature can easily convince anyone that I truly did manage to soften the hearts of many an ancient tyrant.

ELEGANT GiFT FROM OTTOMAN SULTANS

APPEARANCE

LONG SHAGGY TAIL   WEDGE-SHAPED HEAD

MUSCLED YET LEAN, LONG-LEGGED BODY

TEMPERAMENT

Not that I don't like sports, but I've always preferred puzzles and riddles instead. Do you happen to have a well-hidden treat I must first find and then struggle to get out of a hidey hole? Excellent! Would you like to tease me with a mouse wand or entertain me by throwing balls? Great! Then I'll love you, will cuddle you incessantly, and won't leave your side unless you ask me to. Some might think I'm high maintenance, but I'd counter that living with me is a great honor. But don't forget to watch over me—I'm very trusting, even with strangers.

IN WINTER, MY COAT IS THICK WITH A DISTINCT RUFFLE. IN SUMMER, I WEAR A SHORT SILKY COAT, MOSTLY COLORED WHITE

HOW i SAW THE LiGHT OF DAY ←

I come from a region around the Turkish city of Ankara. As early as the 15th century, I started living in the palaces of Ottoman rulers, who began sending me all over Europe as a gift shortly thereafter. I was more voluptuous back then, which earned me fans at royal courts and made me a darling of the cream of European society . . . But woe betide me! I was later unseated by the Persian cat. In fact, my brothers and sisters in zoos were the only reason I even survived the first half of the 20th century! Luckily, I've been kept by many breeders ever since the 1950s.

COLOR DiSPUTE →

To this day, Turkish people still claim that a genuine angora must be snow white, though international cat organizations have been recognizing our black, ginger, and silver forms ever since the 1970s—probably because pure white cats, including Turkish angoras, sadly, tend to be deaf.

EACH EYE CAN BE A DIFFERENT COLOR!

TURKiSH ANGORA COLOR VARiETiES

1. Silver
2. Ginger & white
3. White (traditional)
4. Cinnamon
5. Tri Color (Calico)
6. Black

MEOW NEWS

122nd YEAR — No. 1457 🐾 SINCE 1892 🐾 WEDNESDAY, MAY 28, 2014 🐾 PRICE: 25 CAT HAIRS

LEARNING ABOUT BALANCE WITH ZEN MASTER SHiRONEKO

Body & soul care for cats

Do things sometimes throw you off, dear cat readers? Our editorial team must admit that we know this annoying feeling exceedingly well—for example, whenever we have a bad night or get out of bed on the wrong paw ... Or when our human serves us up with a handful of dry kibble instead of the bowl of chicken liver we've been looking forward to ... Or when we have this horrific feeling that a few unruly hairs are sticking out on our head, even though we've just washed and cleaned ourselves ...

Hello, my name is Shironeko, I'm a Turkish Van, and I would like to welcome you to my course on maintaining inner balance.

If you're suffering from similar issues, don't despair. Here's a picture guide from a certified expert in relaxation and resting—Shironeko, a Japanese Zen master.

1. Let's start by lying on our back and closing our eyes happily. Let your thoughts flow through you like a stream ... Let them come and go ...

2. Now we learn to maintain this state of balance, using three cherry tomatoes. Place one tomato on one paw, the next on your other paw, and the last one on the top of your head. Can you hold this position for longer than 10 minutes, my dear disciples?

3. For advanced students: make this exercise more difficult by building a bell pepper tower...

4. Finally, don't forget to include relaxation in nature in your regimen. To make concentration easier, chant the mantra *"Purr"* ...

That's it! Are you in touch with your inner peace yet? *Purrr* ...

RUSSIAN BLUE

From dirty harbors, I moved all the way to the luxurious chambers of the tsar's palace. Despite my newfound life of luxury, I'm still pretty down to earth.

INTELLIGENCE: Once I learn to open the door, I'll get into your drawers or fetch your ball.

STUBBORNNESS: 🐾🐾🐾

PERSONALITY: Cool bird

INCLINED TO RUN AWAY: 🐾🐾

CUDDLINESS: 🐾🐾🐾🐾🐾🐾

PEACEFUL, MESMERIC ELEGANCE

HOW i SAW THE LIGHT OF DAY

About two hundred years ago, I befriended some sailors in the Russian port of Archangelsk. Brr. If not for them, I would have frozen in the cold streets, dear readers! Later, due to my exquisite beauty and grace, the Russian tsar himself took a liking to me, followed by the English and in due time Europe at large.

TEMPERAMENT

I'm a sociable lady who is very devoted to my owners, though I'm a bit shy. Usually, I take a strong liking to a single member of my colony, but can deign to tolerate the rest. On the other hand, I never say no to some me time, so I don't get sad when my humans aren't home. Overall, I'm a cool bird who loves playing with you—you can teach me how to fetch, if you'd like!

APPEARANCE

BLUISH-GRAY COAT WITH A SILVER SHEEN

ELEGANT STEP DUE TO LONG, SLIM LEGS

TRIANGULAR HEAD WITH EMERALD-GREEN EYES

GUARD HAIRS ARE THE SAME LENGTH AS THE UNDERCOAT, FORMING A THICK, VELVETY COAT

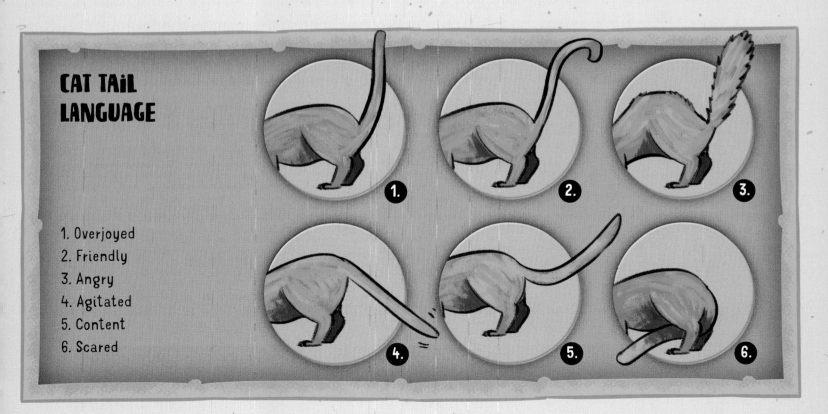

CAT TAIL LANGUAGE

1. Overjoyed
2. Friendly
3. Angry
4. Agitated
5. Content
6. Scared

1.   2.   3.   4.   5.   6.

HiS HiGHNESS VASKA

As I already mentioned, I found my way to the tsar's palace, and most importantly to the tsar's heart. One of my relatives, named Vaska, was beloved by the mighty Tsar Nicholas I himself. But as usual, history is full of twists and my family almost died out in its original homeland during World War II. What a catastrophe, *meow, meow!* Luckily, we didn't disappear completely and today you can find us all over the world.

CAT FOR ALLERGiC PEOPLE (ALMOST)

Do you know what's great about me? I barely shed, and compared to other breeds, my saliva and coat contain only a little bit of "Fel d 1"—a protein and treacherous allergen that makes some people sneeze, scratch themselves, and get teary-eyed whenever they encounter a cat. This doesn't mean that if you suffer from allergies, you can just keep me at home, willy-nilly. I'll still send some of the allergens your way—not on purpose, honestly!

EYES THAT ARE EMERALD . . . YELLOW?!

Nobody, not even other cats, remembers what I looked like when I was still prowling the busy streets of the port of Archangelsk. Likely, my coat used to be thicker (yep, even more so than today). After all, there is talk— at least I hope it's just talk!—that people used to make fur coats out of me. And my famous emerald-green eyes? Oh no, I viewed the world with yellow peepers back then.

MEOW NEWS

80th YEAR — No. 955   •   SINCE 1892   •   THURSDAY, JULY 13, 1972   •   PRICE: 25 CAT HAIRS

MOUSER WANTED

Join the ranks of those protecting the Winter Palace! Do creative meaningful work full-time! On behalf of Her Highness, Catherine the Great, we hereby announce an audition to select 300 of the best mousers from all over Russia. Are you elegant and well mannered? Are your claws fast and sharp? Would you say that you were born to capitalize on this once-in-a-lifetime opportunity? If you answered "yes" to all three questions, then you might be the one we're looking for!

THIS IS WHAT NASTYA WROTE ABOUT WORKING AS A CAT GUARD:

"I was greatly honored to guard the empress herself. It's a job of immense responsibility that allows me to exercise all of my strengths—my elegant gait, my vigilance, and my thoroughness—while hunting. You wouldn't be able to spot even the tip of a mouse tail in the corridors I guard. So, dear lady cats—I can't wait to see you join our ranks! Together, we'll keep the Winter Palace clean, shiny, and free of those mouse troublemakers."

JOB BENEFITS:

Diverse work in the beautiful environment of the Russian Winter Palace. Payments made in rubles or choice cat treats, as negotiated (may be combined). Personal translator (specialized communicator to ensure that the humans fulfill all your needs and requirements). Possibility for career advancement.

Are you a Russian blue cat? Then we give you the exclusive opportunity to guard both the lower and upper floors of the imperial palace. As a bonus, you'll be able to work abroad in other royal courts (such as the United Kingdom), provided that Empress Catherine herself chooses you as a gift for one of her ambassadors! If you are interested, send us your cover letter along with your portrait and paw print by August 13, 1972. Don't forget to add which kingdom you'd like to work in.

SiAMESE CAT

Did I hear you say "Your Highness?" Meow, what is your wish, my beloved human servant?

BLUE-EYED QUEEN

APPEARANCE

TRIANGULAR HEAD WITH A LONG, STRAIGHT NOSE

BLUE EYES

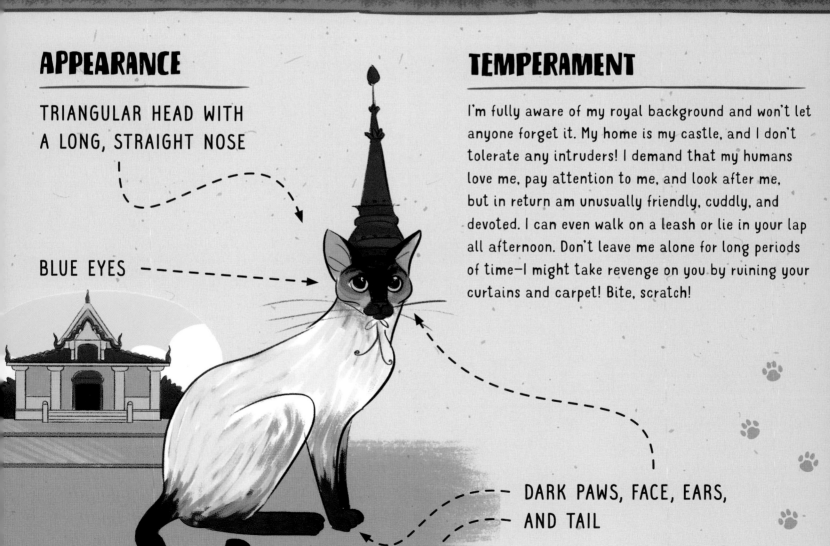

TEMPERAMENT

I'm fully aware of my royal background and won't let anyone forget it. My home is my castle, and I don't tolerate any intruders! I demand that my humans love me, pay attention to me, and look after me, but in return am unusually friendly, cuddly, and devoted. I can even walk on a leash or lie in your lap all afternoon. Don't leave me alone for long periods of time—I might take revenge on you by ruining your curtains and carpet! Bite, scratch!

DARK PAWS, FACE, EARS, AND TAIL

THE REST OF THE BODY IS LIGHT IN COLOR

HOW i SAW THE LiGHT OF DAY

I'm a very old, very noble breed who enjoyed the comforts of palatial life in Siam (now Thailand) all the way back in the 14th century—more than 600 years ago! In Europe, I was admired at one of the first ever cat shows, held in London in 1871.

⬇

TREASURE GUARDiAN

⬆

Some legends say that Thai princesses used to put their rings on my tail—that's why the original Siamese cat had a crooked tail. We are also said to have been loyal guardians of temple treasures, watching them so intently that we became cross-eyed. Well, people may no longer promote our squinty visage, but it was a highly sought-after characteristic 100 years ago!

MEOWY DECiBELS

I'm not shy and will voice my displeasure by meowing loudly. If there's a female Siamese in heat around, trust me—the entire neighborhood will know!

⬅

↑

THAI CAT

Actually, I'm a new breed that looks like the original Siamese—my head is a little wider, my forehead a bit longer and flatter, and my body more robust and muscled than that of my modern relative. But our dispositions are one and the same.

↑

TONKINESE CAT

I was created when the Siamese cat was crossbred with the Burmese cat. I love my human, and I also love toys.

HOW COULD ANYONE GET US MIXED UP?

TOYBOB

I look like a cute kitten and I am nice, cuddly, and obedient. The only thing I lack is a tail, which I don't mind one bit.

↓

BURMESE CAT

Just like the Siamese cat, I too come from Thailand. I am noble and I demand your full attention. For example, I love having endless conversations with you.

↓

MEOW NEWS

13th YEAR — No. 145 SINCE 1892 SUNDAY, JANUARY 1, 1905 🐾 PRICE: 25 CAT HAIRS

HOW MiNOU THE SiAMESE CAT MADE A SAD PAiNTER HAPPY

Pablo Picasso, a rising star of the human art scene, was in very bad shape. Nobody was buying his sad paintings, full of the blue hues of sorrow. Luckily, his loyal Siamese companion Minou put her paw down and decided to knock some sense into the unhappy painter.

"First of all, I took the gentle approach—anytime Pablo showed me a new painting, eagerly awaiting my judgment, I gave a soft unhappy meow and shook my head. But it didn't seem to be working. So I had to do the tough love thing and go for a much more ruthless strategy—I began knocking down his jars of blue paint, one after another ... Every time he so much as looked at yellow paint, cheerful as the sun herself, I purred meaningfully and licked his face. But that didn't work either. I was getting desperate ..."

In an exclusive interview with the Daily Cat, Minou revealed that depression was the reason her human was so sad. Picasso, who was mourning the death of a close friend, spent whole days crying, and that's why his paintings were so glum.

Nobody bought them until things had gotten so bad that the two couldn't even afford food.

"Sure, a cat gets nervous in a situation like this. One day, Pablo showed me an empty bowl and said that he was truly sorry but that I needed to go out into the streets of Paris. That I would have a better life that way. I couldn't take it any longer, so I elegantly dipped my paw in a pink paint, and pressed it right into the middle of a canvas. Only then he finally understood."

To prove that they were buddies through thick and thin, Minou caught a snack out in the streets and shared it with her favorite portrait painter. And wouldn't you know it! The painter perked up, grabbed some pink paint, and his work started selling like crazy. Meow!

~Snow White, editor ~

ORiENTAL SHORTHAIR

A triangular head and looooong erect ears might make me look like an elf from a fairy tale, but my disposition is that of a noble prince.

AN ELF WHO FALLS iN LOVE WiTH YOU

INTELLIGENCE: 🐾🐾🐾🐾🐾🐾
STUBBORNNESS: I love learning flashy tricks . . . on my own terms.
PERSONALITY: Talkative companion
WANDERLUST: 🐾
CUDDLINESS: I love cuddling and having you around, but sometimes need some alone time.

APPEARANCE

TRIANGULAR HEAD WITH A STRAIGHT NOSE AND DISTINCT EARS THAT MAKE THE FACE APPEAR EVEN MORE ELONGATED

GREEN EYES

TEMPERAMENT

Just like my cousin the Siamese, I'm well aware of my noble origins. I'm proud, temperamental, smart, and sociable. You will love and pay attention to me, but in return I will unreservedly adore you and never leave your side for very long. I'm active and curious, and you will never be bored with me. I prefer having a cat companion, and if you get me an oriental friend, you can look forward to us having endless, loud conversations.

SHORT COAT WITH NO UNDERCOAT, FITTING CLOSELY TO A SLIM BODY

DIFFERENT FROM THE SIAMESE

Thanks to my domesticated ancestors, I now come in various colors and patterns: monochromatic, spotted, dotted, marbled . . . even silver. While the Siamese cat has blue eyes, ours are green.

— SIAMESE — ORIENTAL —

HOW I SAW THE LIGHT OF DAY

My lineage is old and famous. After all, I come from the royal breed of Siamese cats. When my ancestors left Thailand and set out into the world in the 19th century, Europeans and Americans fell for them immediately and began cross-breeding them with domestic cats. The natural consequence? A cat which can charm just about anyone, *purrr!*

ORIENTAL CAT COLOR VARIETIES

1. Red
2. Silver
3. Tri Color (Calico)
4. White
5. Blue
6. Black

WITH A LONGHAIR COAT ⬆

Over time, people created a longhair oriental breed. It originated in South America, but its official name is the "Java cat," after the Indonesian island of Java, where the breed never lived . . . Oh, you humans. I don't understand why you make your lives so difficult by coming up with these pointless names . . . These "Java" beauties lack an undercoat (just like me), and so their hairs lie closer to the body and seem shorter than they really are. Try looking into the eyes of an oriental longhair—you might have stumbled upon one with differently colored eyes. For them, that's nothing unusual.

CURIOSITY WON'T KILL THIS CAT

If anyone can be said to be intelligent, it is us, the oriental cats. Not to sound too full of our-selves, but we might even be the most intelligent of all cat breeds. But how does our intelligence manifest itself? By playing, naturally! We love to frolic and come up with new antics, and you wouldn't believe how curious we are. That's why we enjoy exploring the world. And how can we do that if we just lay in our beds and sleep through the day like many other breeds? Not to bad-mouth them, but it's true. Meow, and now leave me alone for a while. I have some exploring to do.

⬇

HOW COULD ANYONE GET US MIXED UP?

⬅ RAAS CAT

I come from the Indonesian island of Rass. I'm bigger than the domestic cat, and I boast a crooked tail.

MEOW NEWS

122nd YEAR — No. 1461 🐾 SINCE 1892 🐾 SUNDAY, SEPTEMBER 14, 2014 🐾 PRICE: 25 CAT HAIRS

STACHE, A CAT STAR WITH A MOUSTACHE

Dear cat lovers! Let us introduce you to the coolest of all cool cats—Stache, a rising cat star. This long-legged mustachioed cat comes from New Jersey and was born in November, the month of mustaches, AKA Movember! Our editorial team stood in line for a very long time before we could talk to this famous oriental cat. Phew! But it was worth it because now you can read the interview our editor Minka did with him.

FROM LEFT TO RIGHT: TEDDY, STACHE, DEXTER, BINDI

Minka: Where did you get such an unusual mustache? Is it a tattoo?

Stache: Not at all. I can guarantee you that my mustache is genuine and completely real. Meow! After all, I was born with it. But others mocked me for it as a kitten.

Minka: That must have been hard . . . It's even rumored that no one wanted to adopt you because they thought you were too—how do I put this?—well, ugly.

Stache: Well, unfortunately you're right. But luckily, one day I was discovered by Christine Gonzales, who loved me just the way I was. She says I'm intelligent, sensitive, and always chic (note: Stache gives us a conspiratorial wink). People in the streets have mistaken me for the famous singer Freddie Mercury, comedian Charlie Chaplin, fictional detective Hercule Poirot, and once even for the cartoon warrior Asterix. Can you imagine?

Minka: There definitely is a resemblance! After all, if a mustache makes the man, why not the cat? I've heard that you live with three other cat fops. Is it true?

Stache: Well, yes. I have a black mustache, my buddy Teddy has huge ears, Dexter looks sort of like a bat, and Bindi has a white dot in the middle of his forehead. Dignity is our middle name in public, but we can be quite the rascals behind closed doors! *Meow!*

Stache

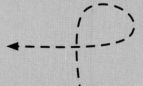

STACHE'S FOOTPRINTS ON THE HOLLYWOOD "PAW OF FAME"

EGYPTIAN MAU

INTELLIGENCE: 🐾🐾🐾🐾
STUBBORNNESS: 🐾🐾🐾🐾🐾
PERSONALITY: Fireball
WANDERLUST: 🐾
CUDDLINESS: Rarely

My true origins are shrouded in mystery. Personally, I'm convinced that cat Pharaohs are my distant ancestors— you know, the ones who ruled Ancient Egypt. Also many modern researchers agree that I'm one of the oldest cat breeds in the world, as I am portrayed inside the Great Pyramids, which were built over 3,000 years ago!

A MYSTERIOUS BEAUTY WITH GOOSEBERRY EYES

MY FACE WHEN
SOMEONE SPOTS ME:
Don't worry, I'm not
touching the sofa ...

EGYPTIAN CAT
AS DEPICTED IN
THE PYRAMIDS

WHAT I DO WHEN
NO ONE'S LOOKING:
Whatever could be beneath
this upholstery?

APPEARANCE

VIGILANT EYES THAT WON'T LET YOU OUT OF THEIR SIGHT (GOOSEBERRY GREEN AND ALMOND IN SHAPE) - - -

SHINY COAT WITH A DOTTED PATTERN

MUSCULAR BODY THAT MOVES LIKE A CHEETAH

TEMPERAMENT

If you want to live with me, you will have to get used to the fact that I make the decisions. In return, I will heroically defend my human till the last breath. I show you my love by sitting next to you and guarding you. When I want to be petted, I ask gently, but firmly. Did you know that I'm the fastest of all cats? I can run at speeds of up to 30 miles per hour!

EGYPTIAN MAU COLOR VARIETIES

1. Black
2. Silver
3. Bronze

MEOW NEWS

1st YEAR — No. 1 SINCE 1892 SATURDAY, DECEMBER 24, 1892 • PRICE: 25 CAT HAIRS

TA-MiU: AN EGYPTIAN CAT PRINCESS

Archeologists discovered dozens of mummified cats in a 2,500-year-old Egyptian tomb. Surprisingly, that wasn't the only thing they found—the cuddly guardians of royal grain often earned their own sarcophagi.

As you surely know, Ancient Egyptians valued cats quite a lot, even worshiped them. One of the ways in which this worship manifested itself was the fact that they provided the exact same post-mortem care to their pets that they afforded themselves—they had them turned into tiny mummies, put them in tiny sarcophagi, and placed a mouse between their paws, just in case the kitty got hungry while traveling to the afterlife.

One such cat, named Ta-Miu, was a pet of the crown prince Thutmose. He truly appreciated his little princess. After all, she would catch mice in royal granaries, and a couple of times even saved his life by killing a venomous snake or scorpion his enemies had planted in his chamber. When Ta-Miu quietly skipped away to the eternal lotus gardens, Thutmose followed a well-established Egyptian tradition and shaved his eyebrows in grief.

We will always remember her witty words, which she sweetly chirped to Thutmose:

> I'm not sure which one of us is about to become the Pharaoh to tell you the truth . . .

TA-MIU'S LIMESTONE SARCOPHAGUS -

ABYSSINIAN CAT

Are you looking for a cat with a capital C? One who tirelessly climbs rooftops and is well aware of her own importance, yet always welcomes you back home with a warm snuggle and a huge heart? Nice to meet you—you've just found her.

INTELLIGENCE: It's said that playful cats are intelligent—meaning I'm a genius among cats!

STUBBORNNESS: 🐾🐾🐾🐾🐾

PERSONALITY: Athlete

WANDERLUST: 🐾🐾🐾

CUDDLINESS: 🐾🐾🐾🐾🐾🐾

CHILD OF THE GODS

APPEARANCE

DISTINCT ALMOND-SHAPED EYES, IN HUES OF YELLOW, GREEN, AND HAZEL

SANDY COAT CONSISTING OF HAIRS THAT CAN HAVE UP TO THREE HUES: WHITE, BROWN, AND BEIGE (WILD RABBITS HAVE SIMILAR COLORS, THOUGH THEY CAN'T HOLD A CANDLE TO ME!)

SOMEWHAT LARGE EARS SET FAR APART

LEAN, NIMBLE BODY ON LONG LEGS

TEMPERAMENT

I'm an energetic, playful, and agile lady. My wild nature is based in high confidence and unceasing curiosity, meaning I'm also very sociable and dignified. Don't forget to give me many opportunities to climb inside your home; otherwise I'll entertain myself with your furniture and curtains. (And knowing full well how you humans are, I bet you wouldn't like that!)

HOW i SAW THE LiGHT OF DAY ↑

Legends say that I used to live in the courts of Egyptian Pharaohs. Whether it's true or not, I've been bestowing the joy of my presence on Ethiopian cat lovers since time immemorial. In the 19th century, British soldiers took me from Ethiopia to England, where I became very popular and began a successful campaign to win the hearts of people all over the world.

ABYSSINIAN CAT COLOR VARIETIES

1. Sorrel
2. Fawn
3. Chocolate

HOW COULD ANYONE GET US MIXED UP?

SINGAPURA CAT ➡

In Singapore, I mostly live on the streets. Sometimes, I even find shelter in sewers. But in the US, where I moved in the 1970s, I've always been a pampered companion.

⬅ CHAUSIE

I came into the world when a house cat was crossbred with a jungle cat. My wild ancestors gave me their love of fast movements and long jumps. *Leeeap!*

SOMALI CAT ➡

I'm the child of the longhair kittens of Abyssinian cats, and now sold as a household pet.

MEOW NEWS

118th YEAR — NO. 1408 · SINCE 1892 · THURSDAY, APRIL 29, 2010 · PRICE: 25 CAT HAIRS

RiDDLE: UNEXPECTED FORTUNE

The Adventures of Sherlock Meows.

Dear curious cats and tomcats (and our human readers and caretakers, of course)! Today, I'm bringing you a riddle to exercise your brain. Naturally, we cats not only care about your comfort, but we also want you to constantly improve and educate yourselves! Are you paying attention yet? I can almost see the smoke rising from your ears!

Once upon a time, there was a lady who was looking after a group of beautiful, rare Abyssinian cats. "One day, I needed to go grocery shopping," she told me. "There was a special offer on tuna—my kitties go crazy for them." I carefully listened to the details of her story. "It was a hot summer day and I opened a window into the garden so that my kitty-cats could enjoy some fresh air." Interesting, I thought and narrowed my eyes, deep in thought. "When I came back, three of the pussycats acted very strange," the lady said, shaking her head. "I began watching them inconspicuously. Each morning, they were very restless. In the afternoon, they would always lie down in the middle of some scrunched-up blankets, even though they used to switch beds. And although they ate the same amount of food as before, they kept getting bigger and bigger . . ."

So, dear readers, can you match my wits and solve this adorable little mystery? What happened to the Abyssinian princesses and how? The answer? As soon as the door slammed shut behind the human lady, one of the local stray tomcats slipped inside through the window. Since then, three of the Abyssinian cats have been carrying tiny kittens in their bellies, hence the morning sickness and the nesting.

THIS IS WHAT ABYSSINIAN CROSSBREED KITTENS LOOK LIKE—BEAUTIFUL, AREN'T THEY?

BENGAL CAT

Even though I may look like a wild beast, I'd love to become your partner in crime. Just allow me to make all the decisions and rules, okay? And come play catch with me!

INTELLIGENCE: 🐾🐾🐾

STUBBORNNESS: I'll always do only what I'm in the mood for—and you can't do anything about it, human!

PERSONALITY: Hunter

WANDERLUST: 🐾🐾🐾🐾🐾

CUDDLINESS: 🐾🐾

A DAREDEVIL THAT ADAPTS

APPEARANCE

ROBUST, BARREL-CHESTED, HEAVY-BONED BODY (I CAN WEIGH OVER 20 POUNDS!)

THE TIP OF MY TAIL IS ALWAYS BLACK

TEMPERAMENT

Hide! Run! Boo, I got you! Can't keep up with me, you say? That's strange, I have energy to spare! I love climbing, running quickly, and hunting anything that moves. I'm no fair-weather cat. Instead, I'm curious, quick to learn, and adventurous. My wild relatives explore the jungle every single day, but you don't need to take me into the wild, oh no. To earn my gratitude, simply put a harness and leash on me and take me for a stroll—to somewhere where there's water, for example. Unlike most cats, I love it. Splash!

FINE COAT WITH AN UN-MISTAKABLE LEOPARD PATTERN THAT SHINES BEAUTIFULLY

SMALLISH HEAD WITH ALMOND-SHAPED GREEN OR YELLOW EYES

HOW i SAW THE LiGHT OF DAY

I'm not exaggerating when I tell you that I was created during a scientific experiment. Really! My grandmother, a wild Bengal cat, was exceptionally healthy. Her kind was even known to never get feline leukemia—that's why scientists wanted to breed her with the house cat to strengthen the health of their shared descendants (humans' furry pets). It took a long time before this breeding produced kittens that could be domesticated, but finally it did. Our unique gene, which prevents us from getting leukemia, fascinates scientists to this day.

BARKiNG CAT

You've never heard me meow, you say? That might be because . . . I don't meow. Instead, I do this strange husky barking. Well, you know, I do have the genes of a predator . . . Have you ever heard a *tiger* meow?

BENGAL CAT COLOR & PATTERN VARiETiES

1. Spotted brown
2. Marbled snow mink
3. Spotted blue
4. Marbled brown
5. Spotted snow mink
6. Marbled blue

HOW COULD ANYONE GET US MIXED UP?

SOKOKE →

I come from Kenya in Eastern Africa, where I used to live in the wild. I'm still a pretty fast runner, and if you upset me, I show my claws immediately!

← OCICAT

I may look like an ocelot, but you wouldn't find a single hint of a wild predator among my recent ancestors. That's because I came to be when the Abyssinian cat was crossbred with the Siamese cat. But I'm still pretty exotic, wouldn't you say?

TOYGER

I may look like a small tiger, but don't worry—unlike a tiger, I always remain a cute playful kitty you love to hold in your arms while falling asleep. Cuddling and snuggling, that's just my thing!

SAVANNAH CAT

Look at my long ears and sheer size! My ancestors include real African predators—servals.

MEOW NEWS

73rd YEAR — No. 869 ❧ SINCE 1892 ❧ TUESDAY, MAY 25, 1965 ❧ PRICE: 25 CAT HAIRS

BABOU
THE OCELOT CAUSES A STiR iN A RESTAURANT

The year is 1965. The place is an unnamed restaurant in Manhattan, New York City

Yesterday's get-together dinner for Babou, a well-known ocelot living with a slightly less well-known painter Salvador Dalí, didn't go as planned.

"Things started off swimmingly," Babou says, scratching his chin. "Dalí decided to introduce me to his friends. Just as they were ordering their food, it seemed as if everything would go off without a hitch. As we approached, I heard them order roast turkey with stuffing and Brussels sprouts with chestnuts, served with a fine sauce. Meooow!" (sad whine—ed. note) So what happened? "One lady saw me, got scared, and began shrieking. She even climbed on her chair." (Babou shrugs his muscular shoulders, puzzled—ed. note) "As if I were a mouse! How humiliating." (Babou scoffs, seemingly disgusted, but his haunted eyes are full of tears—ed. note) And what happened then?

"My buddy said, 'Why are you throwing a fit? He's just an ordinary housecat!' This kind of offended me, but I've forgiven him on account of his good intentions. He went on, saying, 'I painted those spots to make him look prettier!'" (Babou facepalms with his paw—ed. note) "He couldn't have come up with a worse explanation if he had tried."

Clearly, Babou—allegedly given to Dalí by the president of Colombia and accustomed to following his exotic painter everywhere (perhaps with the exception of the bathroom), including voyages on a famous transoceanic liner—was very upset by the whole affair. This is what he'd like to say to the scared lady and others, "Don't be afraid of cats. If you don't spook us and instead give us food and treat us well, we definitely won't scratch or bite you!"

BOMBAY CAT

Grass rustles, a twig snaps, two golden eyes flash in the dark . . . Leap, jump, scratch! Don't worry, it's not a panther—it's me! The mysterious Bombay cat!

BLACK VELVETY JEWEL

APPEARANCE

MUSCLED, ELEGANT FIGURE RESEMBLING THAT OF A PANTHER

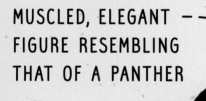

TEMPERAMENT

The truth is, you don't need to worry about accidentally bringing a wild beast home. I may be active, and I may like to frolic and play, but generally speaking I'm a mild-tempered, sociable kitty who loves adults, children, and animals alike and who demands their attention throughout the day. You're lucky that my coat requires a pretty simple type of grooming—long, daily petting!

COPPER OR GOLDEN EYES

BLACK NOSE AND PAWS

BLACK VELVETY COAT

HOW I SAW THE LIGHT OF DAY

I first opened my eyes in the 1950s, in the state of Kentucky. I'm the child of the ordinary American shorthair and the unusual yet elegant Burmilla. Although the first attempts to breed kittens that would look like a large black predator weren't exactly successful, it turned out well in the end. The 1970s even saw me participate in a show for the very first time.

MOWGLI'S TEACHER AND FRIEND

Who doesn't envy Mowgli, the happy and brave boy from Rudyard Kipling's *The Jungle Book* who grew up in the middle of the Indian jungle? The animal that saved him as a baby and stood by his side his whole life was none other than the black panther Bagheera. It was this hero who inspired Nikki Horner, the human creator of our breed. So if you thought that my resemblance to black panthers was just a coincidence, think again!

CAT JUMP iN 4 STEPS

1. Walking casual
2. Preparing to jump!
3. Flying high for
   a while . . .
4. Gracefully landing
   (front paws first)

UNiQUE RARiTY

By now, you surely must be thinking about bringing me home. But wait! We're very, very, very rare. Each year, only a few dozen of us are born in the whole world. We can be owned only by those who can truly take good care of us.

PURRRRRRR!

Unlike other breeds, you won't hear me meowing very often. But that doesn't mean I don't like to talk to you. Quite the contrary! If you make me happy, I can spend pretty much the entire day purring in contentment.

MEOW NEWS

122nd YEAR — No. 1460 🐾 SINCE 1892 🐾 SUNDAY, AUGUST 17, 2014 🐾 PRICE: 25 CAT HAIRS

THERAPY CATS RECOMMEND PURRiNG AS PANACEA!

Some cultures believe that black cats are a bad omen. But today, dear kitties and alley cats, we bring you an interview with two black tomcats who've decided to fight this pernicious myth.

You've had special training to become therapy cats. What does your regular day look like?
Glitter (Missouri, Bombay tomcat): Meow, I've just returned from a classroom full of children who had very poor grades in English. They were reciting Shakespeare, not very well, I might add; they were too shy. No wonder! The teacher was reprimanding and correcting them all the time. I came prepared, though, *purr*, wearing my best suit—a starched collar around my neck, and a goose quill between my teeth! As soon as the kids saw me, all fear and shame melted away. And when I later quietly purred on their laps while they did their reciting, they were perfectly calm. It worked like a charm!

Draven (Pennsylvania, origin unknown): For my part, I spent yesterday riding a pram around a hospital. I jumped into one grandma's bed and helped her exercise her hand—she broke it when she tried to stop a tram with a walking stick. She had her fingers in a cast for a month and they were almost completely numb. But when she petted my back and belly, *purr*, their sense of feeling returned. Soon, she'll be as good as new!

Which qualities must a therapy cat have?
Glitter: They must be fond of humans and always be kind to them . . .

Draven: Meow, precisely! . . . And spread peace, calm, and feline love wherever they go. *Purrr* . . .

CANADIAN SPHYNX

What? I forgot to wear a coat, you say? Meowhahahaha, don't make me laugh! I didn't forget, and I'm not even coming back from a crazy barber. I'm a genuine hairless cat.

WHEN AN ERROR TURNS INTO AN ASSET

APPEARANCE

MY BODY IS COVERED WITH TINY SOFT HAIRS THAT ARE VERY SOFT TO THE TOUCH AND ALMOST INVISIBLE, THOUGH THERE CAN BE NO DEBATE ABOUT MY HAVING A GENUINE COAT

MUSCLED, LEAN, LONG-LEGGED BODY

TEMPERAMENT

Many people are deterred by my unusual appearance. They don't know what they're missing! I'm incredibly cuddly, love my family, and in fact I'm pretty much dependent on them. I love to play and have frequent conversations with you. Too bad you can't understand me ... But you'll never be bored with me. I'm very curious and will go through your shopping bags, wardrobe, and all the nooks and crannies you forgot were in your home (so don't forget to tidy up!) Oh, and I love eating because I need a lot of energy to keep myself warm without a coat. And food is what? Energy, of course! By the way, do you happen to have a snack for me?

DISTINCT CHEEKBONES, ARCHING FOREHEAD, LARGE EARS, DEEP-SET EYES

I LOOK LIKE I HAVE MORE SKIN THAN IS NECESSARY—THAT'S WHY I'M VERY WRINKLY

PRECIOUS SKIN REQUIRES PRECIOUS CARE

Just like you humans, we too need to use sunscreen in the summer and wear a nice jacket in the winter. Our skin also requires weekly bathing to remove the sweat and grease we can't get rid of on our own. As a reward, you can pet me for a long time and enjoy the warmth of my skin. (I'm several degrees warmer than a regular cat.)

HOW i SAW THE LiGHT OF DAY

You might not know this, but hairless cats have been around since time immemorial. The ancient Aztecs, for example, called us "gifts from the gods." But it wasn't until the 1960s that a couple of Canadian breeders tried making a real breed out of us, after their regular black-and-white cat Elizabeth gave birth to a hairless kitten, a black tomcat named Prune. We modern Sphynxes carry not only the genes of grandpa Prune but of many other random naked cats from the US and Canada. And in Russia, our cousin Don Sphynx spontaneously appeared.

CANADIAN SPHYNX COLOR VARIETIES

1. Chocolate
2. White & blue
3. Fawn & chocolate
4. Fawn
5. White
6. Fawn & cinnamon

DECIDUOUS CAT

While some kinds of hairless cats are born hairless, others can't be told apart from their hairy counterparts until they gradually shed their coat. Surprised, are you?

HOW COULD ANYONE GET US MIXED UP?

DON SPHYNX ↑

I come from the Russian port city of Rostov-on-Don, and just like my Canadian cousin I am cuddly, intelligent, and appreciative of heated home where you offer me your loving arms.

↑ PETERBALD

I'm a crossbreed between the Don Sphynx and the Exotic cat. I was born in St. Petersburg, Russia. I don't shed my coat until two or three years of age.

UKRAINIAN LEVKOY ↑

Not only am I hairless, but I also have folded ears and an unusual pentagonal head that looks like a dog's head. And if you think that's odd enough, get a load of this—I love being walked on a leash!

MEOW NEWS

121st YEAR — No. 1450 🐾 SINCE 1892 🐾 SUNDAY, OCTOBER 20, 2013 🐾 PRICE: 25 CAT HAIRS

150-YEAR-OLD TOMCAT: WHAT'S HIS RECIPE FOR LONGEVITY?

Curiosities of the cat world

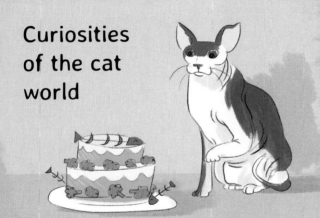

Grandpa is an inconspicuous hairless tomcat of 150 years old, though you would never guess it. Okay, okay—if you squint really hard, you can notice a few tiny wrinkles. But he was born with those, just like any other Sphynx.

His actual birthdate had long been kept from both the human and feline public. Now we know that he was born on February 1, 1964 in Paris. Exactly five years later, he unexpectedly ran off into the busy streets, dodging the wheels of cars. He was saved by a plumber and cat lover named Jake Perry. "What an unusual tomcat! Someone's surely looking for him," thought Jake and put up posters all over the city. They slowly faded, and the

original owner finally made a call. But when she saw how Grandpa got along so well with his new human, she allowed him to stay.

"One day, Jake signed me up for a cat show. I was about 20 then and I won. My opponents meowed unhappily. I even heard someone mutter under their breath, 'What a grandpa!' But I bit my tongue and didn't let it upset me. As a reward, Jake gave me a vanilla cake with broccoli icing and some tuna on top for my birthday."

And what helped him achieve his longevity? "Definitely a healthy diet." He nods sagely. "Each morning, I eat beaten eggs, delicious bacon, broccoli, and asparagus, washing it all down with a hearty gulp of black coffee." You've read correctly, dear readers—coffee! Clearly, Grandpa's diet has been curated, down to the last detail. We can argue about the degree to which it's actually healthy, but by hook or by crook Grandpa has already enjoyed his 34th birthday, which is 150 years in cat years! That earned him an entry into the Guinness World Records, which lists him as the oldest tomcat in the world.

CAT-TO-HUMAN YEARS CONVERTER:

1 year = 15 years

2 years = 24 years

3 years = 28 years

5 years = 36 years

10 years = 56 years

20 years = 96 years

LYKOi

At first glance, I may look like an adorable kitty. But under the full moon, I turn into a bloodthirsty beast, howl at the moon, and search for someone to sink my teeth into . . . Meow, wait, you don't believe me? How dare you! . . . Well, you are right not to. In fact, I'm as closely related to the werewolf as I am to an aquarium fish!

A SMALL WERECAT

APPEARANCE

DON'T BE AFRAID OF ME! I'M NOT ACTUALLY A WERECAT, EVEN THOUGH MY COAT STICKS OUT IN ALL DIRECTIONS AND HAS THE OCCASIONAL BALD SPOT. MY KEEN EYES ARE BRIGHT YELLOW, MY BODY IS LEAN AND AGILE, AND MY LONG TAIL IS UNUSUALLY SHAGGY

MY COAT MAY LOOK ROUGH, BUT IT'S WONDERFULLY SILKY TO THE TOUCH

TEMPERAMENT

When you overcome your fear of me, you'll find that I'm the most loyal, cuddly friend you could imagine. Sure, I tend to be somewhat loud when demanding your attention and affection, but I really do suffer like a dog when no one's attending to me. Children, adults, dogs, or cats—I'll make friends with anyone. The main thing is that I have a buddy to help me avoid any horrible periods of solitude! Meow!

I MAY SEEM CONSTANTLY ANGRY AND NOT LOVING AT ALL, BUT IN FACT THE OPPOSITE IS TRUE!

I'M USUALLY BLACK (PROBABLY BECAUSE BREEDERS ACTUALLY WANT ME TO RESEMBLE A WERE-WOLF AS CLOSELY AS POSSIBLE)

LYKOI OR A WOLF PACK ➤➤

Although I'm a very young breed, I have an old, even ancient name. In Ancient Greek, lykoi means "wolves." So I can confidently claim that I have an entire wolf pack in me, awooooooo!

⬅ WINDOWSILL INSTEAD OF A TANNING BED

People would kill to have my ability to sunbathe! To boast my black coat, all I need is to enjoy a few days in the sun. When I then spend a long period of time away from the heat and sunrays (like in winter), I lose my fur and turn an adorable shade of pink.

CAT FACE EXPRESSIONS

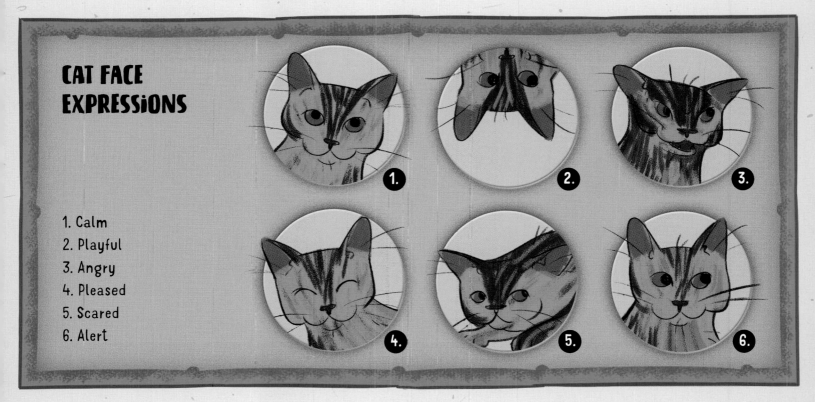

1. Calm
2. Playful
3. Angry
4. Pleased
5. Scared
6. Alert

HOW I SAW THE LIGHT OF DAY →→

If you expect me to have a long, distinguished family history, you're going to be disappointed. In 2010, a Mr. and Mrs. Gobble from Tennessee found a peculiar stray kitten with an irregular, baldish coat. They believed it to be suffering from some kind of a skin disease and had it examined by a doctor. And what a surprise—the kitten was as fit as a fiddle! It wasn't even related to any of the known hairless breeds. I was just an ordinary domestic cat, though one with an unusual genetic mutation. Later, the Gobbles and their successors discovered a few other cats with the exact same gene and managed to crossbreed them. So our breed, which came about in a completely natural way, was stabilized and multiplied by humans.

NEW IMAGE SEVERAL TIMES A YEAR

Do you have a lykoi at home? Have you noticed that when you observe it carefully, it looks a bit different than before? Congratulations, you have a keen eye! My skin cells are twofold. One type can't produce hair, which is why I have bald spots. The other type *can* produce it but doesn't sustain it for long. Meaning, new patches are created while other ones disappear. Do you find me a bit scary now? Hiss!

⬇

MEOW NEWS

126th YEAR — No. 1510 🐾 SINCE 1892 🐾 WEDNESDAY, OCTOBER 31, 2018 🐾 PRICE: 25 CAT HAIRS

ON THE TRANSFORMATION OF A WERECAT COAT WITH WERECAT VINCENT

It wouldn't be autumn if there weren't some spooky stories going around. Today, we give you one such tale. Meet Vincent, a tomcat from the werecat family of Lykoi. The following suspenseful interview was brought to you, dear fans of the *Meow News*, by our editor Minka.

Halloween special

Minka: Welcome, Vincent, meow! When did you first realize you were a werecat? As a kitten?

Vincent: Meow, hello! Not as a kitten, definitely not. To be honest, my siblings and I grew up in the streets as ordinary stray cats. But when I turned about four months old, I started noticing some differences—a darkish coat, snow-white spots on my back, and most importantly, my paws and tail resembled those of a rat or some other kind of rodent.

Minka: Weren't you worried that you were actually a mouse?

Vincent: I myself wasn't worried, but some people got spooked when they saw me, purrr ... My first vet, for example, who screamed, "Yiii, heeeeelp, a ppooooossum!" dropped my carrier box and tried running away. If the nurses hadn't stopped him, he'd still be hurtling around the office.

Minka: Not the most professional, huh?

Vincent: He wanted to send me to the rodent ward, but I held my ground, meow! But then my coat became thinner ... The first shedding period had come. All of a sudden, spots around my ears, shoulders, and tummy were completely bare. Over time, I grew new hairs, which were much lighter and longer than the previous ones.

Minka: Wow! Do you think it could happen again?

Vincent: You bet! We lykois shed our coat several times over the course of our lives. Each time, the new coat can have a different color, length, and thickness! I'm always looking forward to seeing my new haircut!

Minka: You're sort of your own hairdresser! Thanks for the interview and I hope you'll scare many feline and humans on Halloween, being the werecat that you are, *purrr!*

CORNISH REX

I'm a beautiful, unusual, confident wonder with a soft plush coat that I'll gladly allow you to pet before you realize that what I really want is to play with you. Leap and fetch!

INTELLIGENCE: 🐾🐾🐾
STUBBORNNESS: 🐾🐾🐾🐾
PERSONALITY: Eternal kitten
WANDERLUST: 🐾🐾🐾
CUDDLINESS: 🐾🐾🐾🐾🐾 (Have you ever had a cat companion in the bathroom?)

iF THE GREYHOUND WERE A CAT

APPEARANCE

SYMMETRICAL CURLS FORM A SOFT, THICK MAT OF A COAT THAT'S, A BIT ROUGH ON THE BACK – – –

BAT-LIKE EARS ATOP A LARGE NARROW HEAD

EVEN MY WHISKERS ARE CURLY – – –

TEMPERAMENT

I'm the party king of cats! Don't worry, I won't eat your party favors, but you should know that I'm very social, friendly, and outgoing. Wild games, jumping, catching, fetching, rollicking—just my cup of tea! I'm not shy and I like to be the center of attention, especially if it's yours. If I come to the conclusion that a bit of cuddling is in order, I'll come claim my quota of love—*purrr*...

MY LONG TAIL HAS A TIP AT THE END

A LEAN, LONG-LEGGED ELE-GANT BODY THAT RESEMBLES THAT OF A GREYHOUND

HOW COULD ANYONE GET US MIXED UP?

SELKIRK REX ➡

I was born in the Big Sky state of Montana, where a human rescued me from a shelter one day. Some of us come in a longhair versions, but those tend to look like a drowned plush bear. Just take care not to step on me while I'm on the carpet!

DEVON REX ⬆

I was rescued as a stray kitten in the English county of Devon. Unlike the Cornish rex, I'm relatively robust and my ears sit lower on the head. When I give you a serious look, you might get the impression that I'm angry with you, but you'd be mistaken—I'm actually a huge cuddlebug!

HOW I SAW THE LIGHT OF DAY

The credit for my curly coat doesn't go to a permanent hair treatment or to a load of curlers but to a special hereditary gene that people first noticed in 1950 in a countryside kitten in the English county of Cornwall. The kitten's human called him Kallinbunker and tried to create a new breed out of him when her friends asked her to do so—a curly cat, what a sight! But she wasn't successful. If a passionate cat lover from California hadn't taken one of those kittens back home seven years later, the world would have surely lost us forever! In America, people started breeding us with many other cats and succeeded in doing what originally couldn't be done in a small English breeding station—long curly kittens began to be born. Today, we're quite different than our Cornwall great-grandfather. After all, we contain the genes of cats from around the world.

LAMBKIN

I look like the smallest lamb you've ever seen. I came to be when a Selkirk rex was bred with a Munchkin, and well, I'm exactly what you'd think might come out of such a union—a short-legged, totally adorable curlyhead!

⬇

MEOW NEWS

126th YEAR — No. 1511 SINCE 1892 MONDAY, NOVEMBER 12, 2018 PRICE: 25 CAT HAIRS

MEESEEKS: A SMALL WARRIOR WITH A HUGE HEART

Stories with a happy ending

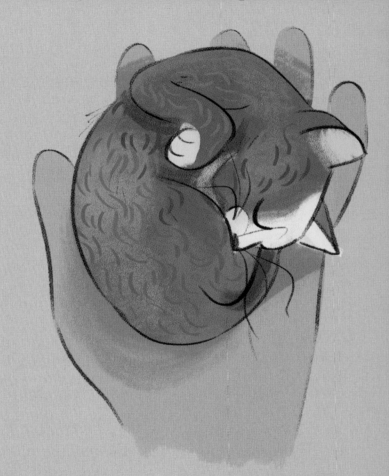

Here's another of our happy stories! This one's about a small but unwaveringly brave daredevil named Meeseeks, who had to use up at least three of his nine cat lives in order to fight his fate.

It's raining ... In the state of Florida, a piteous meowing is coming out of a wet cardboard box sitting next to a dustbin. *Meow, meow!* Quiet voices peep beseechingly. But the unknown person who is hurrying away cares only about not being seen.

The next day, Amanda Kruczynski, who volunteered at the local animal shelter, came to work just like always. Everyone was telling her about the new family of tortoiseshell kittens. Amanda looked into the box, which was now lined with warm soft blankets. The smallest of the kittens, a gray shaggy ball, weighed only half a pound. Unlike his sisters and brothers, he had a curly coat—that's because he was a Devon Rex crossbreed. Without hesitating, Amanda put the entire family into a basket, and took it home, intending to take care of the kittens until they found something more permanent.

"The tiniest one could fit into my palm. He'd always curl up and fall asleep," Amanda showed us. "We've quickly gotten used to one another. Whenever I disappeared behind a closed door, he would shuffle around and wait for me to come back. Playing a loyal guardian earned him the nickname Meeseeks. And when I went to bed, he would paw at my blanket until I made place for him."

But a few weeks later, hard times came for Amanda and Meeseeks. The vet had some bad news for them—Meeseeks was suffering from a serious, possibly fatal disease. Luckily, tiny Meeseeks wasn't intimidated. It turned out that this inconspicuous kitten was quite a warrior and got miraculously better after a week of exhausting treatment.

Once all the rescues grew up a bit, the time came for Amanda to take them to their new homes. But Meeseeks put on such an eloquent protest that Amanda had no other choice but to keep the smallest member of the pack. "All it took was one pleading look and the papers were signed," she smiles.

SUPHALAK

Would you like to have a genuine feline gem at home? Can you afford it? Well, I might know about one such gem—wink, wink!

INTELLIGENCE: 🐾🐾🐾🐾🐾🐾
STUBBORNNESS: 🐾🐾🐾🐾🐾🐾
PERSONALITY: Nag (but no one minds having me constantly around, do they?)
WANDERLUST: 🐾
CUDDLINESS: 🐾🐾🐾🐾🐾🐾

MORE PRECIOUS THAN GOLD

APPEARANCE

A MUSCLED AND PROPORTIONATE BODY, A PERFECTLY SIZED HEAD—NOT A FAN OF EXTREMES, TO BE HONEST

I STAND OUT DUE TO MY BEAUTIFUL CHOCOLATE COLOR, WITH SHADES OF COPPER

MY EYES ARE SAID TO RESEMBLE THE COLOR OF A POMEGRANATE PEEL

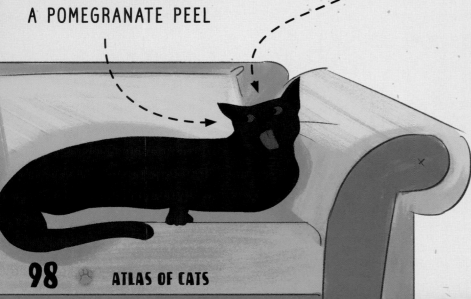

TEMPERAMENT

We Thai cats are naturally loving toward humans, and I'm no exception. That's why I'm always happiest when someone is constantly at home with me. What am I even saying? Being home with me is your duty, and that's that! I'll reward you with my loyalty, protect you wherever you go, and willingly—not to mention loudly—advise you on whatever you're doing. (I'm a well-rounded expert, *meow!*) And cat's honor, I'll do everything in my power to bring you some of that legendary luck. After all, I'm smart enough to come up with something!

HOW i SAW THE LIGHT OF DAY

I'm one of the rarest cat breeds in the world. I come from Thailand. Did you know that Buddhist monks first mentioned me in their writings as long ago as 300 years? Incredible! There's also this rumor about me that I just have to meow to you about: once upon a time, a hostile Burmese king heard that Suphalak cats bring wealth and happiness to people. And because he wanted to be wealthy and happy, he had all of us Thai, chocolate-colored cats moved to his palace. We've been incredibly rare ever since—though I'm not really sure whether we actually brought a happy life to that old scrooge!

HOW COULD ANYONE GET US MiXED UP?

HAVANA BROWN ➡

I'm a friendly, playful, curious, and occasionally impish beauty. If you gaze into my green peepers long enough, I might bewitch you so that you can't live without me!

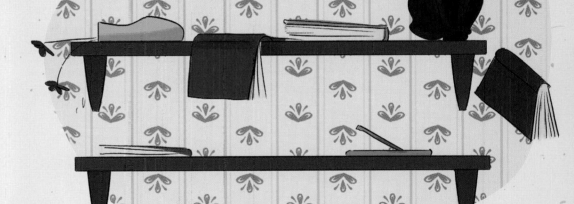

← YORK CHOCOLATE

A long coat and a chocolate color—a perfect combination, don't you think? Cats in fact don't eat chocolate but having a chocolate-colored coat is rare and some would say very chic. Too bad I'm a lost breed now . . . But maybe someone will begin breeding me again someday—perhaps even you?

MEOW NEWS

125th YEAR — No. 1495 🐾 SINCE 1892 🐾 TUESDAY, JULY 18, 2017 🐾 PRICE: 25 CAT HAIRS

SUPHALAK:
THE LOST TREASURE FROM
THE *TREATISE ON CATS*

A view into history

Cats are a treasure, naturally! Purrr ... Certainly, you don't doubt that, dear human readers? If there's still any hint of a doubt knocking around, read a poem about suphalaks, Thailand's national treasure. The oldest ever book on cats, called *Treatise on Cats (Tamra Maeo in Thai)*, says that this ancient breed with a coat the color of warm chocolate is as rare as gold and that anyone owning a suphalak will soon be rich.

An unknown, ancient poet wrote the poem on pieces of tree bark, adding a picture so that anyone who'd read it would know what a genuine feline treasure looks like. Back then, suphalaks were high-ranking members of the Thai royal palace who spent their time giving curious looks to common subjects, who were forbidden from owning them.

But not even such treasures as suphalaks always had easy lives. "In the 18th century, the Burmese-Siamese wars broke out in Thailand," says Professor Meowster, Purr-h.D., a feline historian. "The capital of Ayutthaya, as well as the royal palace with the suphalaks, became shrouded in an impenetrable cloud of smoke. It seemed that the desperately meowing Thai treasure would be lost for good ... Upon his triumphant arrival home, the conquering Burmese king Hsinbyushin busied himself with reading poetry. He learned how rare the suphalaks actually were and sent his entire army back, forcing the soldiers to cover many miles to find the last surviving suphalaks in the city's ruins." Despite this, the breed mysteriously vanished for many years ...

Perhaps that awful experience taught suphalaks to hide somewhere, quiet and scared, and wait for people to start treating them better. And then one person did—Preecha Vadhana, a Thai breeder who managed to regain the trust of these cats by lovingly looking after them. Purrr... Our editorial team has a reason to celebrate—it seems that this chocolate treasure has been saved!

KHAO MANEE

It's been quite a while since I stopped living at the Siamese royal court, but it's still clear that I look like a queen and am worth my weight in gold. (Naturally, my human claims that I'm the most precious thing he has.)

INTELLIGENCE: 🐾🐾🐾🐾🐾🐾

STUBBORNNESS: 🐾🐾 (no worries, I can always entertain myself)

PERSONALITY: Rascal (I can frolic like a small child)

WANDERLUST: 🐾🐾🐾

CUDDLINESS: 🐾🐾🐾🐾🐾🐾

A DIAMOND-EYED QUEEN

APPEARANCE

MY EYES CAN BE BLUE OR GOLD. OR ONE EYE CAN BE BLUE WHILE THE OTHER ONE'S GOLD. THAT'S MY SPECIALITY (ONE THAT BREEDERS FAVOR THE MOST)!

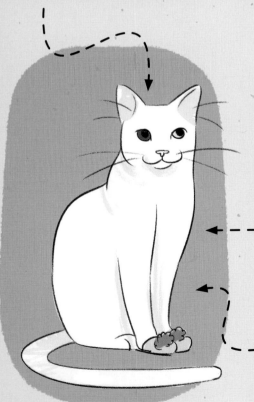

MY MAIN ORNAMENT IS A SNOW-WHITE COAT THAT CONSISTS OF SHORT, SOFT, CLOSE-FITTING FUR

I HAVE AN ATHLETIC, MIDSIZED BUILD

DO I REALLY BRING LUCK?

I sometimes feel like humans like looking for signs and omens where there aren't any. Well, I'm not sure if I can really bring you luck, wealth, prosperity, or longevity like you claim, but I definitely can make your life more joyful.

TEMPERAMENT

I struggle to find any flaw in me to mention. That's probably because I'm no fair-weather friend, I'm loyal to my family, and I greet visitors enthusiastically ("Hi, do you have something tasty for me to eat, and will you keep throwing me this catnip over and over again?"). *Vrrrau* . . . Unlike most cats, you don't need to worry that I'll suffer when left alone. I can easily amuse myself. After all, I can find ways to entertain myself even with you around. I'm quite the daredevil and rascal, you say? Oh come on! Would you prefer to live with a lazy Persian cat instead?

HOW COULD ANYONE GET US MIXED UP?

BURMILLA

I'm nice, friendly, and sensitive. This makes me the ideal feline psychologist, which is why humans often employ me in the field of felinotherapy (sort of a "treatment by cat"—I give you my love and affection to help you heal faster).

SEYCHELLOIS CAT ➡

I'm essentially a Siamese cat with white spots. So expect me to be cuddly, talkative, and highly intelligent, but also jealous and cunning. Dear human, either you'll finally stop petting the neighbor's tabby, or I'll knock down that precious vase you love so much . . . by accident, of course!

HOW I SAW THE LIGHT OF DAY

I'm a very ancient and noble breed. In Siam (modern-day Thailand), poets sang my virtues as early as the 17th century—meow. I always loved to join them! Originally, I was permitted to be kept only on the premises of the royal palace. Nowadays, many other people buy me as well, and not only in my homeland—but they have to dig deep, that's for sure. I don't insist on golden or ivory food bowls but I am very rare. Sometimes, I'm surprised to see how much my precious sisters and brothers have been traveling lately. Finally, we've been getting to know Europe and North America, where the breeding stations may be tiny but are all the more loving.

MEOW NEWS

120th YEAR — No. 1433 ❀ SINCE 1892 ❀ WEDNESDAY, MAY 23, 2012 ❀ PRICE: 25 CAT HAIRS

FUKUMARU: A CAT WITH TWO DIFFERENTLY COLORED EYES

It's morning, the sun has just come up, and not even Misao, an 87-year-old grandmother from the suburbs of Tokyo, Japan, is asleep. Quite to the contrary, she's dancing around the room, grasping a hoe, then grabbing a bunch of seeds, and going out to take a look at how her vegetable patches and flowerbeds are doing. Before crowds of people start swarming the streets, Misao mounts her bike and wheee!! She escapes the hustle and bustle of the metropolis. And what's that in her basket in the back? Why, it's her loyal companion, Fukumaru the tomcat, of course!

One eye yellow, the other one blue—those were the eyes Misao saw when she discovered the kitten in her barn. She named him Fukumaru, or "the ball of fortune" so that fortune would never abandon her. And Fukumaru

has more than earned his name—ever since Misao took him in, he hasn't left her side. They do everything together.

Sometimes, they weed garden beds (the grandma with her hoe, the little tomcat with his paw) or sow seeds. Other times, the garden needs a sprinkling of cold water (Fukumaru doesn't like it but tolerates it). When sunrays hit the back of their necks, they know it's lunch time. But just to make sure, Fukumaru throws Misao a meaningful look that says, "Are you coming, yet? The food's gonna get cold!" Misao smiles, understanding him perfectly. Both of them have poor hearing and prefer to talk with their eyes in order to avoid any misunderstanding. Misao pets the insistent rascal and they sit down to eat. What a wonderful day!

CAT CELEBRITIES

Hamilton the Hipster Cat

Sam the Cat with Eyebrows

Tardar the Grumpy Cat

Princess Monster Truck

Venus the Two-Faced Kitten

TAKING CARE OF A CAT

🐾 Feed your kitty regularly (ideally two or three times a day) and provide access to water. Don't forget that cats are carnivores, meaning that they can't do without meat. Always give her fresh water instead of milk or cream, which she can't digest all that well. And always have a choice morsel at the ready so that you can reward her at any time!

🐾 Clean her litter box.

🐾 Brush her regularly, especially if her coat is thick and long.

🐾 Take her to the vet for her annual check-up. There, she will be carefully examined and vaccinated against diseases.

🐾 Brush her teeth every day, using a soft toothbrush and toothpaste for pets.

🐾 Set up a soft, cozy nook she can have all to herself.

🐾 Play with and pay attention to her every day.

Would you like to do something nice? If you and your parents are thinking about getting a cat, visit your local animal shelter. It's bound to be full of cats, tomcats, and kittens eagerly waiting for someone to give them a real home. One of them is sure to catch your eye!

FELINE RECORD-HOLDERS

Cat with the longest whiskers:
Missi (7.5 iches)

The loudest-purring cat:
Merlin (67 decibels)

The oldest cat:
Creme Puff (38 years: that's 168 in human years!)

The heaviest cat (and the biggest eater): Himmy (46 pounds)

The cat who can do the most tricks: Didga (24 tricks)

The cat with the longest hairs: Colonel Meow

KEEP CALM AND ADOPT A SHELTER CAT!

Helena Haraštová & Jana Sedláčková

Atlas of Cats

Illustrations by Giulia Lombardo

© B4U Publishing for Albatros,
an imprint of Albatros Media Group, 2022.
5. května 1746/22, Prague 4, Czech Republic
Authors: Helena Haraštová & Jana Sedláčková
Illustrations © Giulia Lombardo
Printed in China by Leo Paper Group.

ISBN: 978-80-00-06354-6